The Mark Experiment

How Mark's Gospel can
help you know Jesus better

by
Andrew Page

VTR
Publications

Bibliographic information published by Die Deutsche Bibliothek
Die Deutsche Bibliothek lists this publication in the Deutsche National-
bibliografie; detailed bibliographic data are available in the Internet at
http://dnb.ddb.de.

ISBN 3-937965-21-1

Unless otherwise stated, scripture quotations are taken from the
New International Version.

Cover design: Chris Allcock
Printed in the UK by Lightning Source

Contents

For John and Ruth

I thank God for the many people who have helped me on my journey into Mark's Gospel, especially Christian Bensel, Gerhild and Hans Michael Haitchi, Sven Kühne, Bill and Shirley Lees and Wolfgang Widmann.

I am grateful to Chris Allcock for the drawings and the cover design, and especially to Thomas Mayer of VTR for having the courage to publish the German version of the book in 2004 and now this English edition too.

I thank God for my two home churches in England and in Austria who have prayed for this project: Above Bar Church, Southampton and the Baptistengemeinde in Innsbruck.

Most of all I thank those who have dared to try the experiment for themselves and have experienced the power of Mark's Gospel in their lives. I pray that there will be many more!

http://www.themarkexperiment.com
andrew.page@utanet.at

My Introduction:
Invitation to an Experiment

This is a book about two things at once.

First, it's about learning the Gospel of Mark. I don't think Mark originally wrote his book to be read but to be listened to. After all, most people in the first century couldn't have expected to own a copy for themselves. Mark wrote it so people could memorize it. Not word for word, but bit by bit – so they could get to know Jesus better and tell the story to others.

So, secondly, this is a book about re-discovering Jesus. It's about getting to know him better, loving him and enjoying him. If that's what you want, then you can be sure that Jesus wants you to experience that much more than you do.

So that is what the experiment is about: learning the Gospel so we can get to know Jesus better. I hope you will try it out for yourself.

Please take time to read the rest of this introduction. It won't take you long, but it will help you to get the maximum out of *The Mark Experiment*.

The Structure of Mark

After a short introduction (1:1-8), Mark has divided the Jesus story into six main sections. In the middle of each section is a block of eight incidents which aren't just thrown together anyhow; instead they have their own inner logic.

Look, for example, at Section Two, which runs from Mark 3:13 to 6:6. Here is the structure of the section as I see it.

Block A (3:13-35)

Appointing of the 12 Apostles (13-19)
Opposition from the family (20-21)
Opposition from the religious leaders (22-30)
Opposition from the family again (31-35)

Block B (4:1-5:43)

a	4:1-20	Parable: The sower
b	4:21-25	Parable: The lamp
c	4:26-29	Parable: The seed growing secretly
d	4:30-34	Parable: The mustard seed
d'	4:35-41	Miracle: Stilling of the storm
c'	5:1-20	Miracle: Driving out of Legion
b'	5:25-34	Miracle: Healing of a sick woman
a'	5:21-43	Miracle: Raising of Jairus' daughter

Block C (6:1-6)

Opposition from family and friends (1-6)

There are five things to notice about this structure:

1. Block B has eight incidents with their own inner logic

In this case the eight incidents are arranged in two groups of four: four parables followed by four miracles. Every one of the six sections has a Block B of eight incidents with their own inner logic.

2. Block B has mirror links

Let me explain what this means. The parable of the sower (Incident a) has something in common with the raising of Jairus' daughter (Incident a'), the parable of the lamp (Incident b) has something in common with the healing of the sick woman (Incident b'), and so on. Sometimes there is a lesson from this mirror link; and it is always a help for the memory. And this is true in all six sections of the Gospel.

3. Block A and Block C have something in common

Here in Section Two it's the theme of opposition from the family. This theme isn't there in Block B, but it's a clear link between Blocks A and C. And all the other sections of the Gospel have something linking Block A and Block C.

4. The whole section has a recognizable theme

The theme in Section Two is The Power. In Block B the four parables are about the power of the Word of God, and the four miracles are about the power of Jesus. And every one of the six sections has its own theme.

5. The section can be easily learnt by heart

This is not about learning every word, but simply the order of the events in the section. Most people can learn the order of the events in a section in 10 minutes, especially if they learn Block B before going on to learn Block A and Block C.

But why should I learn Mark by heart?

Good question! But there are some very good reasons:

I.   Because the Bible is the word of God it has remarkable power. We often forget this. In Psalm 119:11 David says to God: "I have hidden your word in my heart that I might not sin against you."

II.   Because Mark has written his Gospel to make this easy! If you read *The Mark Experiment* you will notice how the structure of the Gospel makes learning it by heart very easy. I am sure that the Holy Spirit led Mark to write this way, because he wants us to have his word in our hearts.

III. Because learning the Gospel by heart makes it possible to do Bible study even when you do not have a Bible with you! So while you are lying in bed or walking down the road you can tell yourself the Gospel stories and begin talking to Jesus about what you are remembering.

IV.   Because the first Christians learnt the Gospel by heart. After I had discovered the structure I found this quotation from Clement of Alexandria. Clement is explaining why Mark wrote his Gospel:

> "Mark, the follower of Peter, while Peter was preaching the gospel publicly in Rome in the presence of certain of Caesar's knights…, *being requested by them that they might be able to commit to memory the things which were being spoken,* wrote from the things which were spoken by Peter the Gospel which is called According to Mark."
>
> Clement of Alexandria (Adumbrationes ad 1 Peter 5:13, italics added)

It may seem a strange idea to learn the order of the events in Mark's Gospel by heart. I have written this book because I have tried the experiment myself. And I have rediscovered Jesus!

How to use this book

This book isn't a commentary, it's designed to help you learn the Gospel and so to get to know Jesus better. As we look at the six main sections of Mark there'll be an introduction called *Enjoying the View*: this will explain the logic of Block B and show you what Block A and Block C have in common.

Next comes *Unpacking the Content*. Here I explain how the structure of the section helps us to understand the meaning of the individual paragraphs.

Then I make some suggestions as to how you could memorize the section (this is called *Learning the Gospel*). Most people aren't used to learning by heart, but it really is worth it. And remember we're not talking about learning every word but the order of events in the section. As I mentioned above, most people can do this in about ten minutes.

The last part is called *Meeting the Lord*. This is a reminder of the reason we are doing all this: we want to re-discover Jesus. As you talk to the Lord about what you are learning you will be getting to know him better.

Please don't read **The Mark Experiment** too quickly! You might want to take a week over each of the six sections, so that you have time to learn it thoroughly and begin to experience the Lord using his word in your life. Even if you decide to read everything through in a few days, please come back afterwards and take time to learn the Gospel for yourself – I think this is what the first Christians did, and it's what Mark had in mind when he sat down to write.

Thank you for reading my introduction; now it's time to read Mark's.

I am praying that everyone who reads this book will enjoy Mark's Gospel and enjoy meeting Jesus. The Mark experiment starts now…

Mark's Introduction (Mark 1:1-8)

Mark gives us a very short introduction to his Gospel: he is anxious to get on with the story. In verse 9 Jesus steps on to the stage for the first time, but as an adult and not as a baby. So there is no mention of Mary or Joseph and no account of Jesus' birth. Nevertheless the first eight verses prepare us for the arrival of Mark's main character.

Enjoying the View

a	Mark's witness to Jesus (1)
b	The Old Testament prophets' witness to Jesus (2-3)
c	The baptism of John creates great interest (4-5)
b'	John is like an Old Testament prophet (6)
a'	John's witness to Jesus (7-8)

Mark seems to start his Gospel with an example of mirror linking, which makes the introduction easy to remember. The main purpose of these verses is to introduce us to Jesus before he appears on the scene.

It would be good to read the introduction through two or three times, to pick out what Mark and others say about Jesus. Please take time to worship before we look at the verses in more detail: this book isn't only about information, it's all about re-discovering Jesus and getting to know him better. That's what the experiment is about.

Unpacking the Content

a – Mark's witness to Jesus (1:1)

Verse 1 may be the title to the whole book, but it also tells us what Mark wants our verdict about Jesus to be at the end of the Gospel. Jesus is the Christ, the Messiah God had promised in the Old Testament. Israel had been waiting for centuries for this human saviour; Mark wants us to know that he has come.

But the Messiah Mark wants us to meet is more than just a human being: he is "the Son of God" (1). Although this phrase is not in all the manuscripts, it is almost certainly what Mark wrote. At the end of Section Three, at the halfway stage of the Gospel, Jesus will be recognized to be the Messiah (see 8:29); and in Section Six, near the end of the Gospel, he will be recognized to be the Son of God (see 15:39).

And this, says Mark, is "gospel", good news. Recognizing who Jesus is and why he came is the best thing that can happen to anybody.

b – The Old Testament prophets' witness to Jesus (1:2-3)

"It is written in Isaiah the prophet", says Mark, though he doesn't quote Isaiah until verse 3; in other words, the quotation from Malachi 3:1 in verse 2 is simply an introduction to Isaiah's witness to Jesus.

At this stage we don't know the name of the messenger preparing the way, but Isaiah tells us who he is preparing the way for: "Prepare the way for the Lord" (3). The message is clear: someone is coming who is none other than God himself.

c – The baptism of John creates great interest (1:4-5)

Now Mark tells us that the messenger is John. He prepares the way for the coming of God by preaching about repentance and offering a concrete opportunity to express this publicly – in baptism. Repentance means changing your mind and deciding to live differently from now on, and verse 4 tells us that this is what makes forgiveness possible.

John's message and baptism evokes an astonishing response: "The whole Judean countryside and all the people of Jerusalem went out to him" (5). Clearly there is exaggeration here, but there is obviously huge public interest in John. Surely one reason must be that he was baptising Jews, which was unheard of. Jews need to repent, says John, and it seems as if many were willing to do just this.

b' – John is like an Old Testament prophet (1:6)

Mark's description of John is meant to remind us of Elijah, who wore "a garment of hair and a leather belt round his waist" (2 Kings 1:8). Indeed, Zechariah 13:4 tells us that a hair garment was more or less the prophetic uniform. So this description of John – and the mirror linking – tell us that John is one of the Old Testament prophets, preparing the way for the coming of the Messiah.

a' – John's witness to Jesus (1:7-8)

John makes it clear that he is vastly inferior to the one he is preparing the way for: he is not even worthy to be a slave or a servant and undo his sandals for him (7).

But the really astonishing part of John's message is that the one who is coming "will baptise you with the Holy Spirit" (8). This is extraordinary because in the Old Testament only God can pour out his Holy Spirit on people. With these words John is saying, too, that the one he is preparing the way for will usher in the new covenant. All Jews in the first century knew that God had promised a new covenant (see Jer 31:31-34) and that this would mean that people were forgiven (see Ezek 36:25-27) and had the Holy Spirit living inside them (see Joel 2:28-32). John is saying that the time has come; and the mirror link with verse 1 tells us the name of the one who will inaugurate the new covenant: it is Jesus, the Messiah, the Son of God (1).

Mark's Introduction is designed to get us excited about this Jesus for ourselves.

Learning the Gospel

The mirror linking in these verses makes the Introduction easy to learn. Don't try to learn all the details, just learn the headings.

Meeting the Lord

As you run through Mark's Introduction in your mind, take time to worship Jesus for who he is, and then for what he has come to do. He wants you to know him better and to love him more; ask him to use Mark's Gospel to make those things happen in your life.

Section One: The Message (Mark 1:9-3:12)

Mark has already said that he wants to tell us "the gospel about Jesus Christ, the Son of God" (1:1). The identity of Jesus is central to the message. Now Mark tells us the first thing Jesus says in his public ministry: "The time has come, the kingdom of God is near" (1:15). That is what this first section is about. It is the message everyone needs to hear and it's the message Jesus came to bring.

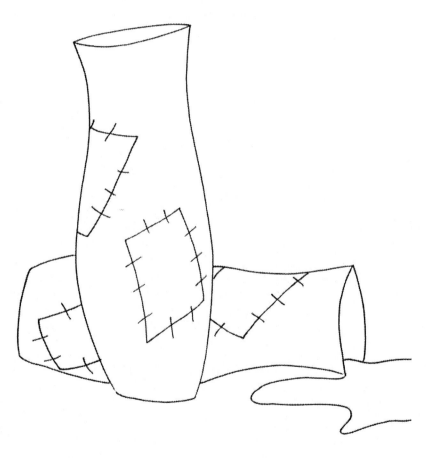

"And no one pours new wine into old wineskins.
If he does, the wine will burst the skins,
and both the wine and the wineskins will be ruined.
No, he pours new wine into new wineskins." (Mark 2:22)

Enjoying the View

Block A (1:9-20)

Baptism and temptation of Jesus (9-13)
Jesus proclaims the good news (14-15)
Jesus calls the first disciples (16-20)

Block B (1:21-2:28)

a	1:21-28	Jesus drives out an evil spirit
b	1:29-34	Jesus heals Peter's mother-in-law and others
c	1:35-39	Jesus says his priority is teaching
d	1:40-45	Jesus heals a leper
d'	2:1-12	Jesus heals a paralytic
c'	2:13-17	Jesus calls Levi and eats with sinners
b'	2:18-22	Jesus predicts a radical break with Judaism
a'	2:23-28	Jesus is Lord of the Sabbath

Block C (3:1-12)

Jesus provokes opposition by healing on the Sabbath (1-6)
Jesus' growing popularity (7-12)

Mark has organized this section – like all the others – around a central block of eight incidents (Block B). The first four show that Jesus is in complete control, liberating people from evil and sickness and committed to teaching the crowds. With Chapter 2, however, the mood changes abruptly: suddenly the Jewish leaders are everywhere, criticizing and finding fault with Jesus – clearly they are feeling threatened by the new competition. So the first half of Block B shows us the authority of Jesus unquestioned by human opposition, while in the second half Jesus is in conflict with the leaders of Israel.

Blocks A and C have, as in all the sections of the Gospel, something in common. Here it is the message that Jesus is the Son of God. In Block A the Father proclaims this at Jesus' baptism (1:11), while in Block C Jesus refuses to allow the evil spirits to announce his identity (3:11). With these signposts Mark is doing two things: he makes clear the beginning and the end of Section One, and he confirms that this is the central message of the Gospel (cf. 1:1).

It might be good to read through Mark 1:9-3:12 before reading further. Take time to worship Jesus as you do.

Unpacking the Content

Block A (1:9-20)

The baptism and temptation of Jesus (1:9-13)

In verse 9 Jesus appears in the Gospel for the first time, but not as authoritative teacher and healer but as a man submitting to John's baptism. For Mark the crucial ingredient is the voice from heaven: "You are my Son, whom I love; with you I am well pleased" (11).

These words of God can be best understood by relating them to words God had already spoken in the Old Testament. At the beginning of the first Servant Song Isaiah lets us hear God's enthusiastic introduction of the servant with the words "Here is my servant, whom I uphold, my chosen one in whom I delight" (Isa 42:1a). But here at the River Jordan God declares "You are my Son", an echo of Psalm 2 (verse 7), which was recognised as a messianic psalm among first-century Jews. There may be an allusion here, too, to God's instructions to Abraham when he told him to sacrifice his son: "Take your son, your only son Isaac, *whom you love...*" (Genesis 22:2).

So readers of Mark's Gospel who know their Old Testament will recognize in this first paragraph of Section One the message that Jesus, baptised by John the Baptist, is the Son of God, the Messiah promised centuries earlier (Psalm 2), and the Suffering Servant (Isaiah 42), who will be sacrificed by his Father (Genesis 22).

The baptism of Jesus makes a huge impact at the beginning of Section One, and Mark surely wants us to see all three Persons of the Trinity here: the Son in verse 9, the Spirit in verse 10 and the Father in verse 11. The message is clear: God himself is intervening dramatically in human affairs.

Mark gives only two verses to the forty days of temptation in the desert (12-13), in contrast to the much fuller accounts of Matthew and Luke. He even neglects to tell us that Jesus triumphed over Satan, probably because he sees this as self-evident. Of more significance is the mention of forty days. Mark may be wanting us to remember Israel's forty years in the wilderness and to conclude that Jesus is the new Israel, God's Son, come to inaugurate a new people of God (see comments on 3:13-19).

Jesus proclaims the good news (1:14-15)

The good news is that "the kingdom of God is near" (15). With the arrival of Jesus God's kingdom is here, not in its ultimate majesty but in the humble reality of individuals acknowledging God as their King. The good news is that it is possible to know God. The condition of entering the kingdom is repentance and faith (15b), which we will understand better by the time we reach the end of the Gospel.

Mark almost certainly has Isaiah 52:7 at the back of his mind as he writes these verses: "How beautiful on the mountains are the feet of those who bring good news, who proclaim peace, who bring good tidings, who proclaim salvation, who say to Zion, Your God reigns!" Jesus is bringing the good news of the kingdom of God.

Jesus calls the first disciples (1:16-20)

The initiative here clearly belongs to Jesus. Simon, Andrew, James and John have perhaps had contact with Jesus for about a year at this stage, but today is to be the day of decision. The call to follow ("Come, follow me") is linked with a promise to equip his new disciples for the task which lies ahead of them ("I will make you fishers of men", 17). Jesus' call, and the response of the fishermen, makes it clear that commitment to Jesus is to take precedence over everything else, including family, possessions and occupation (18, 20).

These are the first four people Jesus has called to come into the kingdom, and they have responded by following him. What other response should be possible, given Jesus' identity (9-11)? In Block A Mark has given us the message about who Jesus is, about the arrival of the kingdom and about his claim on our lives. This is good news for us too.

Block B (1:21-2:28)

Four incidents without human opposition (1:21-45)

a – Jesus drives out an evil spirit (1:21-28)

Jesus performs this first recorded miracle on the Sabbath. But Mark makes sure we see that Jesus begins by teaching (21, cf. 38), and that the subsequent effortless exorcism is the necessary result of an interruption by the forces of evil. These forces, Mark wants us to know, recognize immediately who Jesus is – "the Holy One of God" (24), perhaps a designation for the Messiah. This is a theme we will meet often: people may not know who Jesus is, but the evil spirits experience no such difficulty (see 34b). And they will stop at nothing to prevent God's message being preached.

What the people in the synagogue in Capernaum see clearly is that Jesus is a man with authority, both in teaching and in exorcism. For the first time in the Gospel Mark records amazement as being a natural response to the reality of Jesus (22, 27-28).

b – Jesus heals Peter's mother-in-law and others (1:29-34)

Mark's comment that "they told Jesus about her" (30) may be meant as an encouragement to us to tell Jesus about our worries and concerns. Certainly we are to see that there is no area of sickness or evil which is not subject to Jesus' authority, as the events after sunset make clear (32-34). Mark uses exaggeration ("all the sick and demon-possessed" 32; "the whole town gathered at the door" 33) to paint a picture of human need and desperation finding its answer in Jesus.

Back in verse 25 Jesus had told the evil spirit in the synagogue not to keep revealing his identity; now he repeats the prohibition to the "many demons" he is driving out (34b). The most likely reason for this is that wrong Jewish expectations of a political Messiah who would eject the Romans from Israel for ever would make it very difficult for Jesus to write his own agenda for his ministry. But the next incident shows that this is already a problem.

c – Jesus says his priority is teaching (1:35-39)

This short paragraph shows that Jesus is not willing to be manipulated. Interrupting his praying, Simon Peter's observation that "Everybody is looking for you" seems designed to bring Jesus back to Capernaum, the scene of the previous evening's healings and exorcisms. But Jesus knows that the clamour for miracles will prevent him preaching about the kingdom, so he decides to go elsewhere (38-39). The most important thing is the message.

The mirror link with Incident c' (2:13-17) makes it clear that Mark wants us to concentrate on the purpose of Jesus' coming. Here in 1:38 it is to preach, while in 2:17 it is to call sinners. Of course this does not represent two purposes but one: in his preaching Jesus is calling sinners to repent and believe (cf. 1:15). This is the message of the kingdom of God.

d – Jesus heals a leper (1:40-45)

We do not know exactly what kind of disease the man in verse 40 was suffering from, but it will have isolated him from normal human contact. In any case the man seems sure that Jesus' reputation for having authority over sickness is justified: "If you are willing, you can make me clean" (40). Before replying, Jesus reaches out and touches the man (41). From anyone else, this would be an act of stupidity, but from Jesus it is an act of compassion (41). "Immediately" says Mark, "the leprosy left him and he was cured" (42). Jesus is more infectious than the disease!

The mirror link with the next incident (d', 2:1-12) means we are to see Jesus' submission to the Jewish leaders in 1:44; this contrasts with the Jewish leaders' antagonism to him in 2:7. But the healed leper, commanded by Jesus to tell no one apart from the priest about what has happened, disobeys him. And this disobedience makes it more difficult for Jesus to preach his message (45).

The first four incidents of Block B have shown us Jesus demonstrating his authority and compassion. There is no human opposition but instead constantly growing popularity. The contrast in Chapter 2 could not be greater.

Four incidents with human opposition (2:1-28)

d' – Jesus heals a paralytic (2:1-12)

This is a story Mark enjoys telling. The description of the crowds listening to Jesus teaching the message, its interruption by the opening of the roof and the descent of the paralysed man, make it easy to imagine. The man's friends' determination to bring him to Jesus whatever the obstacles is perhaps meant to remind us of prayer (cf. 1:30); Jesus certainly acts here in response to "*their* faith" (5).

But the surprise here is that Jesus sees a more urgent need than healing. He says to the man "Son, your sins are forgiven" (5). Jesus does not necessarily mean that in this case the man's paralysis is due to specific sin; more probably he means that our greatest need is always forgiveness. This is part of his message.

At this point we meet, for the first time in the Gospel, the opposition of the Jewish leaders. Here it is the teachers of the law, the theologians of the day, who decide that Jesus is blaspheming: by claiming to forgive sin he is doing what only God may do (6).

The answer to Jesus' question in verse 9 is clearly that it is easier to *say* "Your sins are forgiven" than "Get up, take your mat and walk" because the former demands no visible evidence. But now Jesus will say the more difficult sentence and heal the paralysed man physically and visibly, thus proving that he has also forgiven his sins. This double miracle – forgiveness of sin and healing of disease – results in amazement again (12; cf. 1:22, 27).

When he talks about his authority to forgive sins, Jesus refers to himself as the Son of Man (10). This ambiguous expression can sometimes be used to refer to oneself (see for example 8:27 and its parallel in Matthew 16:13); but on the lips of Jesus it often sounds like a claim to be the glorious Son of Man of Daniel 7:13-14, whom all nations will one day worship and whose kingdom (cf. 1:15) will never end. But there is enough ambiguity here so that the crowds, at least, do not catch the reference to Daniel's prophecy.

This incident is important because it shows Jesus forgiving sins and so claiming to be God. Inevitably this results in major confrontation with the Jewish authorities, a theme which will continue throughout the rest of Section One.

c' – Jesus calls Levi and eats with sinners (2:13-17)

Mark begins this paragraph with another reminder that Jesus is committed to teaching his message (13). And now he gives us an account of the calling of another disciple (cf. 1: 16-20). But this is no honest fisherman but a tax collector who has been co-operating with the ruling Romans and cheating his own people. We do not know how much Levi knew about Jesus, but clearly enough to decide to leave everything and to follow him (14).

But the significance of this event for Mark is the reaction of some Jewish leaders to the party at Levi's house, presumably to celebrate his new life and to introduce his new friend. The teachers of the law are here again, and this time they are appalled at Jesus' eating with tax collectors and "sinners" (which may be a euphemism for prostitutes). In the first century, eating with people demonstrated love and acceptance; in their opinion this is disgraceful behaviour on Jesus' part.

The mirror link with Incident c (1:35-39) makes it clear that the significance of this paragraph about the calling of Levi is Jesus' response to the criticism: "It is not the healthy who need a doctor, but the sick. I have not come to call the righteous, but sinners" (17). In both incidents Jesus says that he has come. Probably he is referring to his coming into this world. But Mark wants us to see that Jesus is telling us *why* he has come (1:38; 2:17): to preach his message and to call sinners (cf. comments on 1:35-39). This is what the kingdom of God is about.

b' – Jesus predicts a radical break with Judaism (2:18-22)

Now the conflict with the Jewish leaders intensifies, although Mark does not tell us precisely who it is who comes and asks why Jesus and his disciples do not fast twice a week, as Jewish tradition expected.

In response, Jesus uses three pictures. The first is a wedding (19-20): while the bridegroom is present the guests are hardly going to fast! The second picture is the cloth (21): you don't repair an old piece of clothing with a patch of new material. And the third picture is the wine and the wineskins (22): new wine and old wineskins are a disastrous combination.

Jesus seems to be referring to himself as the bridegroom in verse 19 (though the bride is strangely absent from the picture). In the Old Testament God himself is the bridegroom, never the Messiah; but here Jesus calmly casts himself in the role. It is significant, too, that the bridegroom will be "taken away" (20), an almost violent expression which may be an allusion to the fourth Servant Song in Isaiah 53: "By oppression and judgment he was taken away" (Isa 53:8).

Jesus' comments about new wine and old wineskins are extremely provocative. Ignoring the fact that old wine is normally better than new, Jesus is here describing himself as new wine and the Jewish leaders as old wineskins. It would even be possible to give the first half of Block B the title "New Wine" (1:21-45) and to call the second half of Block B "Old Wineskins" (2:1-28), as the representatives of traditional Judaism make it clear that they cannot accept and welcome Jesus.

Jesus is here predicting a radical break with Judaism. This is a theme which begins here in Section One and is a major factor in Sections Two, Three and Five of the Gospel. We could put it at its simplest by saying that Jesus and religion do not mix. We have to choose. But first there is one more incident in Block B for us to turn to.

a' – Jesus is Lord of the Sabbath (2:23-28)

Mark ends Block B as he began it: with a Sabbath story (see 1:21-28). However, the contrast between the two stories is striking. In the first, the Jewish authorities are nowhere to be seen; in the second the Pharisees are criticising Jesus' disciples for breaking the Sabbath law. A great deal has happened during the course of Block B.

In fact, of course, the disciples are only breaking a traditional Jewish interpretation of the Old Testament Sabbath law. Jesus will return to the issue of the so-called 'tradition of the elders' in Section Three (see 7:1-13; here he teaches authoritatively from the story of David (recalling 1:22, another link with Incident a).

Jesus' most daring statement is in verse 28: "So the Son of Man is Lord even of the Sabbath". This is a direct attack on the authority of the Jewish leaders: for them the Sabbath law was the most important because it was possible to ascertain whether people obeyed it. Jesus is striking at the roots of traditional first-century Judaism.

And so we come to the end of Block B. It is conceivable that the eighth incident should be a double one (2:23-3:6), since both events take place on the Sabbath. But I think, on balance, that the shocking climax of 3:6, to which we will turn in a moment, makes it more helpful to see 3:1-6 as part of Block C.

And in Block B we have come far enough. Mark has structured his story-telling with great care, in order to make clear what he is wanting to stress in each incident, while the massive opposition of the Jewish leaders in Incidents d', c', b' and a' contrasts with the universal approval which greets Jesus' teaching and miracles in Incidents a, b, c and d. And conflict will lead to confrontation.

Block C (3:1-12)

Jesus provokes opposition by healing on the Sabbath (3:1-6)

Mark does not tell us how much time lies between this incident and the one he has recounted at the end of Block B. He paints a dramatic scene, with the Pharisees (whose identity we only discover in verse 6) watching Jesus closely: to heal the man with the shrivelled hand on the Sabbath would be to break their interpretation of the law. (Interestingly they do not seem to be in doubt as to whether Jesus is capable of healing.)

Jesus tells the man to stand up in full view – he is not going to do this in a corner. When the Pharisees refuse to answer his question in verse 4, Mark records his reaction: "He looked round at them in anger and, deeply distressed at their stubborn hearts, said to the man, 'Stretch out your hand'" (5). Jesus' anger and distress lead to a demonstration of power as the man is instantly made completely well.

But Mark has not told us this story for its own sake but because of what follows it in verse 6: "Then the Pharisees went out and began to plot with the Herodians how they might kill Jesus". The Herodians are a political grouping with nothing in common with the Pharisees – except a desire to do away with Jesus. Section One of the six sections of the Gospel is not yet finished but the decision to kill Jesus has already been taken. Mark's expert story-telling is going to keep us reading.

Jesus' growing popularity (3:7-12)

Whether Jesus knows about the plot against him, he withdraws, though the crowds soon find him (7-8). Two important elements in this summary paragraph deserve to be noticed. First, Jesus decides to preach from a boat on the lake (9-10), so that the constant demand for healings does not prevent the crowds from hearing his message. Mark is wanting us to remember 1:38 and is preparing us skilfully for the beginning of Section Two's Block B (see 4:1).

Secondly, Mark reminds us that the evil spirits recognise Jesus as the Son of God (11). As in 1:34 Jesus does not allow them to spread the news (12). But Mark has already let us, his readers, into the secret: in Block C the evil spirits call Jesus the Son of God, and, as Jesus is baptised in Block A, the voice comes from heaven: "You are my Son, whom I love; with you I am well pleased" (1:11).

Mark wants us to reach the same conclusion about Jesus.

Learning the Gospel

The structure of Section One makes it very easy to learn. There is no value in learning the verse numbers; instead, it is better to focus on the headings of each paragraph. The easiest place to start is Block B. Remember that four incidents with no human opposition are followed by four incidents with great opposition.

After you have got the order of Block B more or less in your mind it should be fairly straightforward to remember Block A and Block C – they are both short. It will help you to remember that what Blocks A and C have in common is the phrase Son of God (1:11 and 3:11).

As you learn this first section of Mark's Gospel, you are doing what the first Christians did in the first century.

The Message

| A | Baptism and temptation of Jesus
Jesus proclaims the good news
Jesus calls the first disciples | 3 |

| B | a Jesus drives out an evil spirit
b Jesus heals Peter's mother-in-law and others
c Jesus says his priority is teaching
d Jesus heals a leper | 1 |

| | d' Jesus heals a paralytic
c' Jesus calls Levi and eats with sinners
b' Jesus predicts a radical break with Judaism
a' Jesus is Lord of the Sabbath | 2 |

| C | Jesus provokes opposition by healing
    on the Sabbath
Jesus' growing popularity | 4 |

A+C: Who is Jesus? – Son of God (1:11 / 3:11)

Logic B: four events without and
              four events with human opposition

Meeting the Lord

Once you have got the order of events clear, you can begin to allow the Holy Spirit to use the Jesus story in your life. As you start to tell the events of the section to yourself, be ready to begin praying. Thank Jesus that the message of the kingdom of God is about his gift of forgiveness (2:5) and his love for sinners (2:17). And remember that Jesus is the Son of God. I pray that you will begin to worship as you remember this message. You will be meeting the Lord.

And as you re-tell Mark you will re-discover Jesus.

Section Two: The Power (Mark 3:13-6:6)

The message of Section One was that in the coming of Jesus God is intervening dramatically in human affairs. The Son of God shows his authority and continues, despite opposition, to reach out in love to suffering men and women. Now, in Section Two, Mark explains how this is possible: where does the power come from which changes lives?

"The farmer sows the word." (Mark 4:14)

Enjoying the View

Block A (3:13-35)

> Appointing of the 12 Apostles (13-19)
> Opposition from the family (20-21)
> Opposition from the religious leaders (22-30)
> Opposition from the family again (31-35)

Block B (4:1-5:43)

a	4:1-20	Parable: The sower
b	4:21-25	Parable: The lamp
c	4:26-29	Parable: The seed growing secretly
d	4:30-34	Parable: The mustard seed
d'	4:35-41	Miracle: Stilling of the storm
c'	5:1-20	Miracle: Driving out of Legion
b'	5:25-34	Miracle: Healing of a sick woman
a'	5:21-43	Miracle: Raising of Jairus' daughter

Block C (6:1-6)

Opposition from family and friends (1-6)

Once again Block B has eight ingredients, and once again they can be divided into two groups of four. The first four are four parables told by Jesus, the second four are four miracles performed by Jesus – again it is obvious that Mark has structured the section very carefully.

What Block A and Block C have in common is the theme of opposition. In Block A Jesus' family want to forcibly take him home because he is "out of his mind" (3:20-21). In Block C Jesus is teaching in his home town Nazareth, and his family reject his message. And Jesus says "Only in his home town, among his relatives and in his own house is a prophet without honour" (6:4). These two signposts mark the beginning and the end of Section Two.

Another theme common to both blocks is that of power. In Block A the teachers of the law accuse Jesus of performing exorcisms by the power of Satan (3:22), while in Block C Mark tells us that Jesus "could not do any miracles there, except lay his hands on a few sick people and heal them" (6:5).

Block B will answer the question as to where the power comes from which can change people's lives and bring them into the kingdom of God.

The four parables teach us that the power is in the word of God, while the four miracles teach us that the power is in the person of Jesus himself.

Before we look a little more closely at the text, it is worth mentioning that Section Two contains the first examples of a so-called Mark sandwich. Mark likes to start a story or take up a theme, and then interrupt it with something else, before coming back to it again. This breaks up the rhythm of the narrative somewhat and builds tension. It also makes it easier to learn. The two examples here are in Chapter 3:20-35 and in Chapter 5:21-43.

This might be a good opportunity to read the whole of 3:13-6:6 in order to get a feel for the structure. It is only a short step from reading to worship.

Unpacking the Content

Block A (3:13-35)

Appointing of the 12 Apostles (3:13-19)

Near the beginning of Section One Jesus called his first disciples (1:16-20); now at the beginning of Section Two he chooses twelve out of all those who are already following him. They are to spend time with him (14), and then to be sent out with two main tasks: to preach and to drive out demons (14-15). Once again this is Jesus' initiative.

What is very significant here is the number of apostles. It seems particularly provocative on Jesus' part to choose twelve. He has already signalled a radical break with traditional first-century Judaism (see 2:18-22), and some of the leading Jews have already decided that they must be rid of him (3:6). At the beginning of his ministry Jesus has spent forty days in the desert (1:13), which may be an allusion to Israel's forty years in the wilderness. And now Jesus chooses twelve apostles. Are they to replace the twelve tribes of Israel and to be the foundation stone of a new people of God? Mark does not answer the question here but the theme will return dramatically in Section Five.

Opposition from the family (3:20-21)

Mark tells us that Jesus' growing popularity means that Jesus and his disciples are not always able to eat regular meals. His family's reaction is that "he is out of his mind" (21); they decide to come and take him home.

This short paragraph is the beginning of a Mark sandwich on the theme of opposition (20-35).

Opposition from the religious leaders (3:22-30)

The teachers of the law have presumably come down from Jerusalem specially to give their considered theological opinion about Jesus. He is either possessed by Satan or at least under occult influence (22). This is where he gets his power.

So Jesus tells them that their position is illogical: why would Satan use Jesus in order to arrange the downfall of his own evil kingdom (23-26)? And now Jesus explains what is really happening in his exorcism and healings: "No one can enter a strong man's house and carry off his possessions unless he first ties up the strong man. Then he can rob his house" (27). The picture is clear. The devil is like a strong man who holds people in his power as his own possessions. What is happening in the events of the Gospel is that Jesus is overpowering Satan in order to set people free. In Block B we will meet a dramatic example of this (5:1-20).

Jesus now attacks his attackers (28-30), by teaching about the blasphemy against the Holy Spirit. These Jewish leaders are not ignorant of the facts about Jesus or about the Old Testament promises about the Messiah: by accusing him of having an evil spirit controlling him (30), they are sinning against the truth – knowingly and deliberately. For this sin against the Holy Spirit, says Jesus, there is no forgiveness.

This seems to contradict the Bible's teaching elsewhere that God gladly forgives any who repent of their sin and trust him. The solution to the puzzle is surely that those who have committed the blasphemy against the Holy Spirit never repent and ask for forgiveness. This is not an ignorant sin but a deliberate one; and it is not *any* deliberate sin, but deliberately and knowingly ascribing the truth and light of God to Satan's lies and darkness.

So the person who worries that she may have committed this sin has not committed it; if she had, she would be supremely unworried. And one more thing needs to be said here: we do not have the right to decide at what point someone has committed this irrevocable sin. Not even Jesus does that here – he is not telling the teachers of the law that they have already reached the point of no return, he is warning them that this will happen if they persist in their deliberate rejection of the truth.

Opposition from the family again (3:31-35)

Now the family have arrived and want to speak to Jesus; this completes the Mark sandwich begun in 3:20-21. Jesus responds by making clear that he has a new family: "Whoever does God's will is my brother and sister and mother" (35). He is referring to the new people of God, of whom the twelve Apostles are the beginning (13-19).

This opposition to Jesus in Block A must have made some of these newly-chosen apostles wonder if Jesus could really be from God: why are the people who know him best (his family) and the people who know the Scriptures best (the teachers of the law) rejecting Jesus? The first ingredient of Block B will give us the answer.

Block B (4:1-5:43)

Four parables about the power of the word of God (4:1-34)

a – The parable of the sower (4:1-20)

Jesus has already arranged for a boat to be available (see 3:9) and now he uses it so that he can teach the crowds on the shore (1-2). Mark makes clear in verse 2 that he is only recording some of Jesus' parables here in Chapter 4 (cf. Matthew's seven parables in the parallel passage in Mt 13).

In verse 13 Jesus states that the parable of the sower is the most important: "Don't you understand this parable? How then will you understand any parable?" The first reason this parable is so vital is that it is about listening to the word of God. Already in its telling Jesus says "Listen!" (2a) and "He who has ears, let him hear" (9). And the explanation in verses 14-20 is very specific: "the word" is mentioned in every verse. The parable is about how we hear what God has to say to us.

The second reason this parable is paramount is that it explains the opposition which Jesus faces and of which we have already had a taste in Block A. Why doesn't everyone rush to receive Jesus? Because there are four kinds of human heart, says the parable: hard hearts (15), superficial hearts (16-17), overfull hearts (18-19) and open hearts (20). In other words the disciples are not to be surprised if Jesus is rejected – it is to be expected. Whenever the word of God is taught we should expect disappointment and fruit: disappointment at the opposition and fruit as people recognise Jesus and his claim over their lives. This is a lesson disciples should never forget.

But how are we to understand verses 10-12? Does Jesus mean that God does not want people to turn to him and be forgiven? The answer to that question must be No. Jesus tells the disciples in verse 11 that there are two groups of people: the outsiders, who do not understand and so reject God's message, and the insiders, who may not understand but who ask Jesus to help them (see 10, 34). The parables are not an intelligence test but an openness test, designed to show to which group each listener belongs. Spiritually open people are hungry to know more and so ask Jesus for help. This is still true today.

There is one part of the parable of the sower which Jesus does not explain in verses 14-20. "The farmer sows the word" (14), but who is the farmer? Is Jesus talking about God sowing the message or about us, his disciples, sowing the message? The answer is almost certainly "Both!" But, who-ever shares the message, the power to change lives is in the word of God.

b – The parable of the lamp (4:21-25)

In this second parable Jesus is comparing the word to a lamp. The teaching of God's message reveals what kind of people we are and whether we are really spiritually open or not. If I am not really listening I will soon no longer understand the small amount of God's word which I have so far grasped; but if I am open to God I will understand more and more (25). So powerful is the word of God.

c – The parable of the seed growing secretly (4:26-29)

Only Mark records this parable for us: it perfectly fits his theme in Block B. Jesus again emphasizes the power which the word of God contains. After the seed has been sown there will definitely be growth and this growth is not dependent on the sower: "Night and day, whether he sleeps or gets up, the seed sprouts and grows, though he does not know how" (27).

Jesus is encouraging discouraged disciples. When the word of God is sown, growth is certain: "All by itself the soil produces corn" (28). And the harvest is certain too, as verse 29 makes clear. So there is no secret ingredient which produces growth when the word of God is sown, says Jesus: the power is in the word itself.

d – The parable of the mustard seed (4:30-34)

The message here is more or less the same as with the previous parable. But now Jesus emphasizes the power in the word of God in two ways: first, he chooses the smallest known seed in the first century, to teach the apparently insignificant beginnings when the message of the kingdom is taught. And, secondly, "it grows and becomes the largest of all garden plants" (32). The fact that "the birds of the air can perch in its shade" (32) may indicate no more than the considerable size of the full-grown plant. In any case Jesus is absolutely confident that the kingdom of God will grow, because the word of God has so much power within it.

We must not look far in order to discover why Mark records precisely these parables from the many known to him (33). Four parables – to be followed by four miracles in 4:35-5:43 – make sense in the structure Mark has chosen for his Gospel. And in all four parables Jesus is teaching us about the power of the word of God.

Four miracles about the power of Jesus (4:35-5:43)

d' – The stilling of the storm (4:35-41)

Why has Mark chosen these four miracles for the second half of Block B? The answer is not hard to find. They show us the power of Jesus at work in every area of life: over nature (4:35-41), over evil (5:1-20), over sickness (5:25-34) and over death (5:21-43). If Jesus is Lord in these four areas in which we human beings constantly experience our powerlessness, then he is Lord over everything. The ramifications, as the disciples are beginning to see in 4:41, are frightening and overwhelming. If we take a closer look at this first miracle, this will become all the clearer.

Mark paints a very vivid picture of the ferocity of the storm (37). The disciples, who include four experienced fishermen well used to Galilee and its weather, think it a real possibility that the boat will sink and that they will all drown (38). Probably they are surprised that Jesus is managing to sleep through it all; presumably they wake him because they consider a miracle necessary and possible.

Mark now shows us Jesus absolutely in command of the situation. There are at least two surprises in verse 39: first, Jesus speaks to the wind and waves with words one might use to stop a dog jumping up: "Quiet! Be still!" And, secondly, nature obeys him. It is astonishing enough that the wind holds its breath, but the waves disappear at once rather than taking some time to subside: "It was completely calm." For Jesus this is in one sense nothing remarkable: "He said to his disciples, 'Why are you so afraid? Do you still have no faith?'" (40)

By means of his structure Mark has linked this miracle with the parable of the mustard seed. Like the mustard seed, the question as to the identity of the man in the stern (41) is a very small beginning; but with this overwhelming miracle and the question it prompts Jesus has started a process which will lead not only to the disciples recognising who Jesus is but to millions of men and women down the centuries being changed by the power of Jesus. As I write these words and as you read them, many of us are part of this "largest of all garden plants" (32).

c' – The driving out of Legion (5:1-20)

Mark seems to link this miracle and the parable of the seed growing secretly with a purely verbal connection: the phrase "night and day" appears in Mark's Gospel only in 4:27 and 5:5. But there is more here. Evil is constantly at work to destroy human beings (see 5:5), but the kingdom of God is constantly growing (see 4:27). And this incident will show us which is stronger.

Again Mark emphasizes the impotence of the people to restrain the powers of evil rampant in this man (1-5): "No one was strong enough to subdue him" (4). It is a terrible picture of the destructive powers of sin and evil. Once again the demons recognize who Jesus is (7) and a strange conversation follows in which Legion seems to negotiate with Jesus about what should be done with him, asking to be sent into the pigs.

Many questions spring to mind at this point but they must not be allowed to deflect us from Mark's main message. The powers of evil can only do what Jesus allows them to do – and they recognize that fact: "He gave them permission, and the evil spirits came out and went into the pigs" (13a). Evil is no match for the majestic power of Jesus.

The response of the people to this miracle is fear (15b, cf. 4:41), not because they have lost their pigs but because of the indisputable evidence of what Jesus can do in someone's life: "they saw the man … sitting there, dressed and in his right mind, and they were afraid" (15). They are frightened of Jesus and his power.

Jesus does not allow the liberated man to come with him: he is to tell his family what God has done for him (19) – though words would surely be unnecessary after such a radical transformation! On this occasion Jesus is not commanding silence (as, for example, in 1:44, and later in 5:43), presumably because this is a Gentile area (1, 20 – Jews would not have been allowed to keep pigs) and so the people would have no misconceptions about the Messiah because they would probably have no preconceptions as to how God through the Messiah might break into human history.

Mark ends his account by recording that the man begins to tell the story of what Jesus (not God) has done for him (20). Whether the man himself has recognized that Jesus is God is perhaps doubtful. What is certain is that Mark intends us to get the message: the astonishing power of Jesus to change lives is nothing less than the power of God. This is the answer to the disciples' question in 4:41.

b' – The healing of a sick woman (5:25-34)

This miracle is the middle of a Mark sandwich, an interruption to the progress of Jesus on his way to heal Jairus' daughter. Once again Mark stresses the impossibility of the situation: the woman has been suffering from internal bleeding for twelve years, and many doctors have only succeeded in making her condition worse (25-26). So she is seriously ill, ritually unclean, extremely poor and desperately lonely. She comes up behind Jesus in the crowd, touches his cloak and is immediately healed (27-28).

Now, says Mark, listen to this: Jesus has so much power that people are healed even without his deciding to heal them! The power of God pulses through his personality as surely as the blood flows through his veins.

But Jesus knows that something has happened: "At once Jesus realised that power had gone out of him" (30b). Despite the disciples' incredulity in verse 31, Jesus is determined to find out who, of all the people touching him in the crowd, has touched him deliberately. And he waits until the woman comes and tells him "the whole truth" (33). For the second time in the Gospel Jesus is seen to be responding to faith (34, cf. 2:5).

This extraordinary – because unintentional – healing by the power of Jesus should fill us with awe. But Mark wants us to see something else too. The structure of Block B links this miracle (b') with the parable of the lamp (b, 4:21-25). It is easy to think of the woman's healing when reading 4:22: "For whatever is hidden is meant to be disclosed, and whatever is concealed is meant to be brought out into the open." This is exactly what Jesus does in 5:30-34, and it is what his power wants to do in our lives, too.

a' – The raising of Jairus' daughter (5:21-43)

The mounting desperation of the synagogue ruler (22) must have made Jesus' conversation with the woman almost unbearable for him; and, sure enough, the news comes that his daughter has died (35). But Jesus turns to Jairus with the words "Don't be afraid; just believe" (36).

It seems that Jairus is ready to take Jesus at his word – he does nothing to dissuade him from continuing the journey. Perhaps the woman's faith has strengthened his own. And when Jesus arrives at the house and says "Why all this commotion and wailing? The child is not dead but asleep" (39), it is not Jairus and his wife who laugh in mocking disbelief, but the others who have gathered to mourn the dead girl.

Mark links this incident with the parable of the sower (a, 4:1-20). Whenever God's word is proclaimed, there will always be different reactions: some will laugh and reject the message, but some will believe.

But let us return to Jairus' house. In 4:39 Jesus had spoken to the weather; now in 5:41 he speaks to a dead girl – and she obeys: "Immediately the girl stood up and walked around" (42). Jesus, typically, tells them to keep this miracle quiet; and, realising the depth of their astonishment (42), reminds them that the little girl is probably hungry (43).

Mark's message could not be clearer. The power of Jesus is so great that nature, evil, sickness and even death must obey him. There is no situation in which Jesus is out of his depth. This is an invitation to bring our problems to him and to trust his divine power.

The structure of Block B and Mark's masterly story-telling have answered the question as to how human lives can be transformed. The parables tell us that the power is in the word of God; the miracles tell us that the power is in the person of Jesus. And there is no division between the two: it is Jesus who speaks the word of God in 4:1-34 and it is his words which bring transformation in the miracles of 4:35-5:43 (see 4:39; 5:8, 34, 41). Mark is surely inviting us to believe in him.

Block C (6:1-6)

Opposition from family and friends (6:1-6)

Mark's short conclusion to Section Two returns us to the world of scepticism and opposition. Jesus is in Nazareth, where he had lived as a child; later he had moved to Capernaum (see 2:1). But when Jesus preaches in his home synagogue he is met with cynical amazement: "Isn't this the carpenter? Isn't this Mary's son and the brother of James, Joses, Judas and Simon? Aren't his sisters here with us?" (3) And Mark explains what this means by adding "And they took offence at him" (3b).

Jesus knows exactly what principle is at work here: "Only in his home town, among his relatives and in his own house is a prophet without honour" (4). And so, in a striking contrast to the works of power in Block B, "he could not do any miracles there, except lay his hands on a few sick people and heal them" (5). After so many people have been astonished by Jesus (see 1:22, 27; 2:12; 5:20, 42), now it is his turn to be astonished by them – or rather by their lack of faith (6).

So Section Two ends with disappointment. As Section One ended with the religious leaders plotting his downfall (3:6), so Section Two ends with opposition from those who think they know him best.

Learning the Gospel

Section Two is easy to learn. Start with Block B again: it won't take more than a few minutes to learn the four parables and then the four miracles. Don't worry about all the details – you can include more of these after you have grasped the basic outline.

Block A and C should then present few problems. Remember that the theme of the family's rejection can be found in both. The extra ingredients of Block A are the calling of the apostles, and the Jewish leaders' rejection of Jesus in the middle of a Mark sandwich.

Please do take the time to learn the section: I am sure that the first Christians did. The better we know the Gospel, the better we shall know Jesus.

The Power

| A | Appointing of the 12 Apostles
Opposition from the family
Opposition from the religious leaders
Opposition from the family again | 3 |

| B | a Parable: The sower
b Parable: The lamp
c Parable: The seed growing secretly
d Parable: The mustard seed | 1 |

| | d' Miracle: Stilling of the storm
c' Miracle: Driving out of Legion
b' Miracle: Healing of a sick woman
a' Miracle: Raising of Jairus' daughter | 2 |

| C | Opposition from family and friends | 4 |

A+C: Opposition

Logic B: four parables – power of the word
four miracles – power of Jesus

Meeting the Lord

As you take opportunities to run through Section Two in your mind you will find yourself praying and worshipping. You may want to pray about your experience of sharing the good news with others as you re-tell the parables of Block B: ask the Lord to help you not to be surprised when your message is rejected, but ask him to help you expect that some will respond positively, too.

And you will be moved to worship as you re-live the miracles of Block B. Look at Jesus' authority in every area of life; share the astonishment of some in the crowd; and ask him to demonstrate his power in you and through you today.

I pray for you that as you re-tell Mark you will re-discover Jesus.

Section Three: The Training (Mark 6:7-8:30)

So far in the Gospel the disciples have had plenty of opportunity to witness Jesus' words and works of power, and they have started to wrestle with the question "Who is this man?" (4:41) But to a large extent they have been spectators, watching and listening. Now, in Section Three, Jesus will involve them much more as he trains them in discipleship and in recognising who he is (8:29).

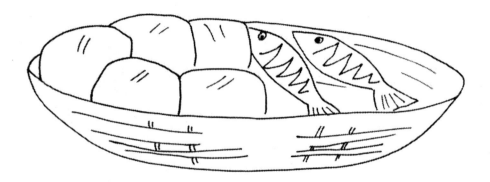

"They all ate and were satisfied." (Mark 6:42)

Enjoying the View

Block A (6:7-33)

Jesus sends out the Twelve (7-13)
The death of John the Baptist (14-29)
The Twelve return to Jesus (30-33)

Block B (6:34-8:10)

a	6:34-44	Feeding of the 5,000
b	6:45-52	Jesus walks on the water
c	6:53-56	Jesus heals in Gennesaret
d	7:1-13	God's word and human tradition
d'	7:14-23	What makes people unclean?
c'	7:24-30	Jesus and the Syro-Phoenician woman
b'	7:31-37	Jesus heals a deaf and dumb man
a'	8:1-10	Feeding of the 4,000

Block C (8:11-30)

The Pharisees demand a sign (11-13)
The confusion of the disciples (14-21)
The healing in two stages of a blind man (22-26)
Peter's confession of Jesus (27-30)

Mark's central block of eight incidents (Block B) begins and ends with the miraculous feeding of a vast crowd. In both cases Jesus involves the disciples, as part of their training. In the middle of the block, in Incidents d and d', Jesus attacks two elements of traditional first-century Jewish teaching: the tradition of the elders and the issue of what makes people unclean before God. These two incidents are the hinge on which the whole of Block B turns: in Incidents a, b and c Jesus has three encounters with Jews, while Incidents c', b', and a' describe three encounters with Gentiles. So there is both a clear development and an inner logic to the structure of Block B.

Once again, Blocks A and C have something in common. Here it is the key personalities of John the Baptist and Herod. In Block A Mark recounts the story of John's death at Herod's instigation (6:14-29). In Block C, when Jesus asks the disciples for the crowds' assessment of who he is, one of the answers is John the Baptist (8:28). And intriguingly, Jesus warns the disciples a little earlier about "the yeast of the Pharisees and of Herod" (8:15). Matthew, in his parallel passage, has "the yeast of the Pharisees and Sadducees" (Mt 16:11); here, Mark seems to be deliberately providing signposts to signal the beginning and end of Section Three.

There are two Mark sandwiches in this section. The whole of Block A comes into this category: the report of the death of John the Baptist is sandwiched between the sending out of the disciples and their subsequent return (6:7-33). Fittingly, the second sandwich can be found in Block C. Mark tells the story of the healing in two stages of a blind man (8:22-26); before this he records the confusion of the disciples (14-21), and after it their conviction, at last, that Jesus is the Messiah (27-30).

Before we turn to the text in more detail, please take time to read Mark 6:7-8:30 for yourself. You may want to ask the Lord to be training you, as he was training the first disciples then.

Unpacking the Content

Block A (6:7-33)

Jesus sends out the Twelve (6:7-13)

Near the beginning of Section One Jesus called his first disciples (1:16-20); at the beginning of Section Two Jesus chose the twelve apostles (3:13-19); and now, as Section Three begins, he sends them out on a training mission. As we noted above, a Mark sandwich starts here.

Jesus' instructions in verses 8-10 are designed to make it necessary for the disciples to depend on God to provide for all their needs. If they and their message are not welcomed in any village, Jesus tells them to "shake the dust off your feet when you leave" (11), a sign that the people's response is not the disciples' responsibility.

The apostles do three things on their mission: they preach the necessity of repentance (12), they perform exorcisms and they heal many people (13). But something else is happening too. Instead of simply listening to and watching Jesus they are now learning by doing. This is a key part of Jesus' training of his disciples.

The death of John the Baptist (6:14-29)

Mark tells us this story in a detailed way, but it is a curious fact that this incident is not in the correct chronological order: John has almost certainly been dead for many months at this stage in the Gospel.

So the question arises as to why Mark chooses to tell us about John's death now. His sandwich (7-33) tells us the answer. Although Mark focuses on Herod's guilty fears and bad conscience in verses 16-29, the wider context of verses 7-13 and verses 30-33 makes it likely that he is wanting to tell us something about discipleship. The apostles' mission (7-13) appears from verse 13 to have been a success; when they return to Jesus (30-33) they will have been glad to tell him what they have experienced (see 30). But Mark wants us to know that discipleship has its price. John the Baptist was a faithful follower of Jesus: "John had been saying to Herod 'It is not lawful for you to have your brother's wife'" (18). But John's faithfulness cost him his life (26-29).

So this is Mark's message in Block A: we must not be naïve about what following Jesus means. The disciples experienced the power of God as Jesus sent them out with his authority (7), but disciples will sometimes experience persecution and even death for the sake of Jesus and the gospel.

The Twelve return to Jesus (6:30-33)

Mark completes the sandwich by recording the end of the training mission: "The apostles gathered round Jesus and reported to him all they had done and taught" (30). In his concern for them Jesus sees their need of food and rest (31-32), but this is denied them by the persistence of the crowds (33). Discipleship, Mark has told us in Block A, has a positive and a negative side.

Block B (6:34-8:10)

Three incidents involving Jews (6:34-56)

a – The feeding of the 5,000 (6:34-44)

This is the only miracle of Jesus recorded by all four Gospel writers, and in addition Matthew and Mark report the feeding of the 4,000 (see 8:1-10). What is so important about the feeding of a vast crowd of people?

The answer is to be found in the prophecy of Isaiah in the Old Testament. In a passage looking forward to the end of time, Isaiah writes as follows: "On this mountain the Lord Almighty will prepare a feast of rich food for all peoples, a banquet of aged wine – the best of meats and the finest of wines. On this mountain he will destroy the shroud that enfolds all peoples, the sheet that covers all nations; he will swallow up death for ever. The sovereign Lord will wipe away the tears from all faces; he will remove the disgrace of his people from all the earth. The Lord has spoken" (Isa 25:6-8). Today we would call this a poetic description of heaven; Jews in the first century called this great feast the messianic banquet, at which the Messiah himself would be the host.

The feeding of the 5,000 is, of course, not the messianic banquet, but it is a preview. Jews who knew their Old Testament prophecy would think immediately of Isaiah chapter 25 and see this miracle as an indication that Jesus is the promised Messiah. In the fourth Gospel John records that after witnessing this miracle people tried to force Jesus to become a political king (Jn 6:14-15). We can notice, too, in passing, how Jesus responds to the needs of the crowd. Mark writes: "When Jesus landed and saw a large crowd, he had compassion on them, because they were like sheep without a shepherd. So he began teaching them many things" (34). The remedy for the lostness of the crowd is not miracle, but teaching. What men and women most need is to hear the truth about themselves and about God.

But let us return to the miracle. Jesus deliberately uses the situation as an opportunity to train the disciples. When they tell him to send the crowds away so that they can buy food, Jesus calmly replies "You give them something to eat" (37a). The disciples explain to Jesus "That would take eight months of a man's wages!" (37b), at which Jesus underlines the impossibility of the situation by asking them to find out how much food they have available – five loaves and two fish!

Jesus is deliberately putting the disciples in a position in which they are out of their depth. He has already done this in Block A (see 7-13), and here he is doing it again. Part of their training must be to see their own inability to cope alone, without God, and to see that the word "impossible" is not in God's vocabulary.

Jesus involves the disciples again as the miracle is taking place: "Taking the five loaves and the two fish and looking up to heaven, he gave thanks and broke the loaves. Then he gave them to his disciples to set before the people" (41). This is the same principle at work again: the disciples are no longer mere spectators; they are learning by doing. The disciples are being trained to be involved in Jesus' purposes and to recognize who he is.

At the end of the paragraph Mark underlines the immensity of the miracle by telling us that, after everyone had eaten enough "the disciples picked up twelve basketfuls of broken pieces of fish and bread" (43). When I invite friends for a meal, there is less food at the end than at the beginning; with Jesus it is the other way round!

b – Jesus walks on the water (6:45-52)

Now Jesus exposes the disciples to a different kind of training experience. This miracle is not one in which they are actively involved – until, that is, Peter asks if he may walk on the water too. (But Mark chooses not to record Peter's request.) This miracle is unusual in the Gospel of Mark as one directed only towards the disciples. They are not witnessing something which Jesus is doing for others; he is doing this for them. This is training too.

Mark tells us in verse 52 that "they had not understood about the loaves; their hearts were hardened". So this miracle seems to be designed to prepare the disciples to recognize who Jesus is. Indeed, just before Jesus climbs into the boat he calms their fears by saying "Take courage! It is I. Don't be afraid" (50). In the Greek "It is I" is "I am", the name by which God had revealed himself in the Old Testament (see, for example, Exodus 3:14). But the disciples still do not get the message.

c – Jesus heals in Gennesaret (6:53-56)

"As soon as they got out of the boat", Mark tells us, "people recognized Jesus" (54) – something the disciples have yet to do in the fullest sense. This summary paragraph paints a picture of Jesus effortlessly meeting human need wherever he encounters it. Mark adds, in a sentence reminiscent of 5:27-29, "They begged him to let them touch even the edge of his cloak, and all who touched him were healed" (56). What are the disciples thinking as they witness all this? How close are they getting to the truth about Jesus? We shall have to wait till Block C to find out.

Two attacks on traditional first-century Judaism (7:1-23)

d – God's word and human tradition (7:1-13)

Although the issue of ritual uncleanness is the reason for Jesus' teaching in these verses, it is not until verses 14-23 that he addresses it directly. Here, in verses 1-13, Jesus explains to the Jewish leaders that their position on the issue is a symptom of a much deeper problem. This is a crucial subject and a key part of the disciples' training.

In the opinion of first-century Jews there were two sources of divine revelation: the written word of God and the oral tradition handed down from one generation to the next. This second source was known as "the tradition of the elders" (3, 5). Jesus accuses the Jewish leaders of not recognizing that the oral tradition was of purely human origin. Even worse: "You have let go of the commands of God and are holding on to the traditions of men" (8). In other words they are ignoring God's word in favour of man-made ideas. To make the point Jesus resorts to sarcasm: "You have a fine way of setting aside the commands of God in order to observe your own traditions!" (9) And this, he adds, is not a new phenomenon: Isaiah prophesied about it when he declared that "their teachings are but rules taught by men" (7).

Jesus gives an example of what this means in practice. The Old Testament law made it clear that people were to honour father and mother (10), but there was a tradition of the elders which taught that it was not necessary for an adult child to provide financial support for parents in need, provided the child's money had been declared "Corban", dedicated to God (see verses 10-12). Jesus summarizes the situation like this: "Thus you nullify the word of God by your tradition that you have handed down" (13). And, sadly, this is not an isolated example: "And you do many things like this" (13b).

Jesus is not attacking human tradition in itself, but as soon as this is given the same authority as the word of God, then in practice it replaces it.

These verses are a massive attack on the Jewish leaders from Jerusalem (1). Before Jesus quotes Isaiah's words "These people honour me with their lips, but their hearts are far from me" he tells them that Isaiah "prophesied about you hypocrites" (6).

But, interestingly, Mark tells us nothing about the reaction of these leaders (though perhaps we can imagine how they may have felt!). The focus in Section Three is on the training of the disciples. They are there, listening (2,17), and learning that human tradition – however positive – must never be allowed to contradict the word of God.

d' – What makes people unclean? (7:14-23)

Now Jesus turns to the specific issue of what causes people to become dirty and unclean before God. Jewish tradition in the first century taught that it was external contact with sin and sinners which was the root cause; Mark has already given us an example of this attitude earlier in his Gospel (see 2:15-16).

But Jesus makes it clear that it is the sin in our hearts which makes us unclean before God, and not external influences: "Nothing outside a man can make him 'unclean' by going into him. Rather, it is what comes out of a man that makes him 'unclean'" (15).

In verses 17-23 Jesus is alone with his disciples. He is teaching them that the human heart is evil: "For from within, out of men's hearts, come evil thoughts, sexual immorality, theft, murder, adultery, greed, malice, deceit, lewdness, envy, slander, arrogance and folly. All these evils come from inside and make a man 'unclean'" (21-23). If we do not believe this we shall think we can save ourselves by our own efforts. As Jesus had said at Levi's party, "I have not come to call the righteous, but sinners" (2:17).

Three incidents involving Gentiles (7:24-8:10)

c' – Jesus and the Syro-Phoenician woman (7:24-30)

The first three incidents of Block B (Incidents a, b and c) involved Jews; now, after Jesus' criticism of traditional first-century Jewish teaching in Incidents d and d', Mark ends the block with three incidents involving Gentiles (Incidents c', b' and a').

The disciples, of course, have already seen Jesus demonstrate his love to a Gentile (see 5:1-20); and now, once again, he is moving to a Gentile region (24). However, his reaction to this Gentile woman looks to be anything but loving: "First let the children eat all they want, for it is not right to take the children's bread and toss it to their dogs" (27). The comment is not as harsh as it seems. In the first century Jews used to talk of Gentile dogs, but Jesus uses a different word here, referring not to the wild animals in the street but to the pet dogs in a family. Nevertheless he is making clear that, at this stage in God's plan of salvation, Israel has priority. The significant thing about the woman is that she accepts this, but still asks for help: "'Yes, Lord', she replied, 'but even the dogs under the table eat the children's crumbs'" (28). Jesus, in turn, responds to the woman by healing her daughter – and without the girl even being present!

b' – Jesus heals a deaf and dumb man (7:31-37)

Jesus now returns to the region in which he had driven out Legion (31, cf. 5:20). Of the four Gospel-writers only Mark tells us this story. Jesus' actions in verses 33 and 34 help the deaf and dumb man to believe that he may be about to experience a miracle, which is what happens in verse 35.

"People were overwhelmed with amazement", Mark tells us (37), as were the disciples in the corresponding Incident b after Jesus had walked on the water (see 6:51). "He even makes the deaf hear and the dumb speak", they say (27b), which is almost a quotation from Isaiah 35:5-6 about the coming of the Messiah. These are Gentiles – they do not know the Old Testament scriptures; but without knowing it they are recognizing who Jesus is.

a' – The feeding of the 4,000 (8:1-10)

If this miracle, like the feeding of the 5,000 in 6:34-44, is a preview of the messianic banquet, it is particularly significant because the people here are Gentiles. First-century Jews, for the most part, had assumed that the banquet would be for Israel alone, and yet the prophecy from Isaiah quoted earlier had promised "a feast of rich food for all peoples" (Isa 25:6).

Once again Jesus involves the disciples and underlines for them the impossibility of the situation. After the disciples have distributed the food, Mark tells us: "The people ate and were satisfied. Afterwards the disciples picked up seven basketfuls of broken pieces that were left over" (8).

If we are surprised that the disciples seem to have forgotten the first miracle (4), we will see in a moment that Jesus is surprised too at how slow they are to grasp the truth.

The structure of Block B has shown us Jesus training his disciples so that they will learn to serve him and to recognize who he is. In the tense encounter with traditional first-century Judaism in the middle of the block, the disciples have learnt three things: that religious people can sometimes be hypocrites, that the word of God is higher than any human tradition, and that the human heart is hopelessly corrupt. But they are still not quite sure who Jesus is.

Block C (8:11-30)

The Pharisees demand a sign (8:11-13)

We might well think that Jesus has given enough evidence in his miracles and teaching of his authority and identity, but here the Pharisees demand a supernatural sign from heaven. But Jesus refuses to help those who are determined to be spiritually closed. "Then he left them", Mark tells us in verse 13. Of course this is meant physically, but there may be a deeper meaning here, too.

The confusion of the disciples (8:14-21)

Jesus warns the disciples not to allow themselves to be influenced by the Pharisees and Herod (14-15). What does he mean? We have seen the Pharisees' major mistake in Incidents d and d' in Block B of this section: their traditions have become more important than the word of God. This is a constant danger for disciples. Helpful traditions (e.g. a "Quiet Time" every day) can become more important to us than the Bible itself. And another aspect of the yeast of the Pharisees is the demand for proof, in other words the refusal to believe (see 8:11-13).

And what does Jesus mean by the yeast of Herod? The extended story of the beheading of John the Baptist in Block A tells us the answer. In 6:17-20 Mark tells us that Herod enjoyed listening to John and protected him, "knowing him to be a righteous and holy man" (20). But then he makes his rash promise to Herodias' daughter, who then, urged on by her mother, demands John's head (25). Immediately we read this: "The king was greatly distressed, but because of his oaths and his dinner guests, he did not want to refuse her" (26). The yeast of Herod is to disobey the word of God out of fear of how others may react if we obey it.

So we have here a key part of the training of the disciples: "Watch out for the yeast of the Pharisees and that of Herod" (8:15). Our own traditions and our fear of others can prevent us from being faithful followers of Jesus.

But Jesus realises that the disciples are deeply confused: they think he is talking about bread! And he is perplexed: "Do you have eyes but fail to see, and ears but fail to hear?" (18), and he goes on to give them a short memory test about the details of the miracles. But they are still unclear and confused about the identity of the man who performed them: "He said to them, 'Do you still not understand?'" (21).

The healing in two stages of a blind man (8:22-26)

As we saw at the beginning of Section Three, this healing is the central section of a Mark sandwich which began in verse 14 and will end in verse 30. This is a very strange incident: the other Gospel-writers may have decided not to record it because it could so easily be misunderstood. We simply do not know why the healing takes place in two stages.

But from the context we do know what conclusions Mark wants us to draw. Spiritual sight rarely arrives in an instant; coming to see who Jesus is and what this means for us is a process, during which Jesus is gradually opening our eyes to the truth we need to see. In verse 25 Mark writes these words: "Once more Jesus put his hands on the man's eyes. Then his eyes were opened, his sight was restored, and he saw everything clearly".

This is not a process which is finished when someone has become a Christian. Disciples should never make the mistake of thinking they know Jesus enough; the most important aim of his training is to open our eyes so that we see him more clearly.

Peter's confession of Jesus (8:27-30)

With the end of the sandwich we arrive at the climax of Section Three. Now we will find out how much progress the disciples have made in the training programme Jesus has been leading them through.

Caesarea Philippi, almost on Israel's northern border, is in a region in which very little happens; it is as if Jesus is hanging a notice on the door saying "Please do not disturb". Now, after hearing the crowds' assessment of his identity, Jesus comes to the crunch question: "'But what about you?' he asked. 'Who do you say I am?'" (29)

The word "you" in Jesus' question is plural: he knows the disciples have been discussing things among themselves. So Peter answers on behalf of all of them: "You are the Christ" (29). This reply is extraordinary: Jesus is the Saviour promised by God long ago in the Old Testament. Peter and his friends have been watching, listening, wondering and learning; spiritually speaking, Jesus has been putting his hands on their eyes (cf. 25) – and now they can see.

The training of Section Three is now complete – although the disciples still have a lot to learn. Mark has finished the first half of the Gospel and he surely wants us to imagine Jesus turning to us and asking "Who do you say I am?"

It is one of the most important questions we will ever be asked and the answer we give will change our lives forever.

Learning the Gospel

Once again, begin with Block B. Mark has made it easy for us: remember that the block begins and ends with the feeding of a huge crowd. In Incidents d and d' we see Jesus confronting first-century Jewish religion. Before this there are three encounters with Jews and after it three encounters with Gentiles.

The sandwiches of Blocks A and C make them easy to learn, too. Remember that the theme of Section Three is training and it will make sense more quickly. I am sure that Mark wrote his Gospel to be learnt; and I am sure that you will enjoy it once you begin!

The Training

| A | Jesus sends out the Twelve
The death of John the Baptist
The Twelve return to Jesus | 4 |

| B | a Feeding of the 5,000
b Jesus walks on the water
c Jesus heals in Gennesaret | 2 |

| | d God's Word and human tradition
d' What makes people unclean? | 1 |

| | c' Jesus and the Syro-Phoenician woman
b' Jesus heals a deaf and dumb man
a' Feeding of the 4000 | 3 |

| C | The Pharisees demand a sign
The confusion of the disciples
The healing in two stages of a blind man
Peter's confession of Jesus | 5 |

A+C: Herod (6:14 / 8:15)

Logic B: d, d': confrontation with the Jewish authorities
            a, b, c: encounters with Jews
            c', b', a': encounters with Gentiles

Meeting the Lord

You might try going for a walk and talking to the Lord about all that he does in Section Three to train the disciples and open their eyes. I think you will find yourself thanking him, and you will find yourself worshipping as you realise that he is at work in your life too.

For if you have recognized that Jesus is the Messiah, this is because he has been opening your eyes. But there is still so much more to see! Ask him to help you avoid the yeast of the Pharisees and of Herod and, above all, to help you to see him more clearly.

For this Gospel is not just about Jesus and the disciples in the first century; it is about Jesus and you in the twenty-first.

I pray that you will meet Jesus again as you talk to him.

Section Four: The Cost (Mark 8:31-10:52)

The disciples have recognised who Jesus is (8:29), but they still have a great deal to learn. In Section Four Mark shows us Jesus performing only two miracles and spending much more time alone with his disciples. His teaching answers two questions. What will it cost Jesus to bring men and women the forgiveness of sins? And what will it cost disciples to follow him?

"If anyone would come after me,
he must deny himself and take up his cross and follow me."
(Mark 8:34b)

Enjoying the View

Block A (8:31-9:29)

First prediction (8:31-33)
The call to discipleship (8:34-9:1)
The transfiguration (9:2-13)
Jesus drives out an evil spirit (9:14-29)

Block B (9:30-10:31)

a	9:30-32	Second prediction
b	9:33-37	"I am the greatest"
c	9:38-41	"We are the only ones"
d	9:42-50	"Sin doesn't matter"
d'	10:1-12	Attitude to marriage
c'	10:13-16	Attitude to children
b'	10:17-27	Attitude to possessions
a'	10:28-31	The rewards of discipleship

Block C (10:32-52)

Third prediction (32-34)
James and John's request (35-45)
The healing of blind Bartimaeus (46-52)

As this section contains three similar predictions by Jesus of his death (10:45 is somewhat different), Mark has decided to use a prediction to start each block. Once again, Block B has a clearly identifiable structure: Incidents b, c and d summarize three mistakes disciples can easily make, while Incidents d', c' and b' introduce us to three areas in which disciples of Jesus must be radically different from the world around. Again, Mark has structured the section very carefully.

What links Block A and Block C (apart from the first and third predictions) is the theme of following Jesus. In 8:34 Jesus tells the crowd "If anyone would come after me, he must deny himself, take up his cross and follow me". And in the last verse of Section Four, at the end of Block C, Bartimaeus, now able to see Jesus, begins to follow him (10:52).

Although there is an emphasis in Section Four on the cost of discipleship there is another element to look out for. What motivates Jesus to go to the cross and what can motivate disciples to follow him is the certainty of future glory (see, for example, 9:2-8, 41; 10,29-30, 37).

With all this in mind, this would be a good opportunity to read through the whole of Section Four, in order to get a sense of the structure. Feel free to stop reading sometimes, to worship and to pray.

Unpacking the Content

Block A (8:31-9:29)

The first prediction (8:31-33)

Mark has chosen his words very carefully in verse 31: "He then began to teach them that the Son of Man must suffer many things..." In the first three sections of the Gospel Jesus has not spoken openly about his death; only now, because the disciples have finally grasped that he is the Messiah (8:29), can Jesus start to explain to them what kind of Messiah he is going to be. The glorious Son of Man (cf. Daniel 7:13-14) *must* suffer, not because the Jewish leaders are stronger than he is, but because this is God's plan for the salvation of the world.

But Peter is having none of it: he "took him aside and began to rebuke him" (32). Jewish expectations of a political Messiah who would liberate his people from Roman occupation were taken for granted in the first century, and Peter understandably shares them. But it does seem extraordinary that, having just recognized Jesus as God's promised Saviour, he now proceeds to tell him how he is to fulfil God's will.

Jesus' rebuke of Peter is shocking: "'Out of my sight, Satan!' he said. 'You do not have in mind the things of God, but the things of men'" (33). This has clearly been a temptation for Jesus: humanly speaking he must want to avoid the cross. But it is possible that the beginning of verse 33 tells us how Jesus was able to resist the temptation: "But when Jesus turned and looked at his disciples, he rebuked Peter." Only Mark's Gospel includes the detail that Jesus looked at them all before rebuking Peter. It could be that Peter never forgot this and passed the memory on to Mark. Jesus, by looking at his disciples, is reminding himself that his friends can never be forgiven if he refuses to die. His love for them is what gives him the strength to go to the cross.

The call to discipleship (8:34-9:1)

Now the focus moves from the cost to Jesus to what it will cost disciples to follow him. Jesus is talking to the crowd now, too (34), and the message is clear: disciples who follow a suffering Messiah must expect to suffer themselves. It hurts to deny oneself – to refuse to live a self-centred existence; and people who take up a cross are accepting the possibility that they will face a martyr's death. This is what following Jesus means.

In verses 35 and 36 Jesus tells us why it makes complete sense to take this radical step. The best explanation of this comes from Jim Elliott, who was martyred in 1956 when he tried to bring the gospel to the Auca Indians of South America: "He is no fool who gives up what he cannot keep, to gain what he cannot lose."

Now Jesus warns his listeners about the consequences of being ashamed of him and his words: "The Son of Man will be ashamed of him when he comes in his Father's glory with the holy angels" (38). It is worth noting here that Jesus sees himself as more than the Son of Man; by talking about coming in "his Father's glory" he is also calling himself the Son of God (see 1:11; 3:11).

The most obvious interpretation of Chapter 9, verse 1 (see the commentaries for a full discussion) is that Jesus is referring to his transfiguration, which will be a preview of his glorious coming at the end of time. Mark seems to make the connection, because he tells us nothing about what happened in the days between verses 1 and 2.

The transfiguration (9:2-13)

Jesus' clarity in talking about the cost of the kingdom, both to himself (8:31-33) and to those who want to follow him (8:34-38), might have given the disciples pause for thought about their decision. In any case the memory of this revelation of Jesus' divine glory will give Peter, James and John the courage to press on, however great the opposition might be.

Moses and Elijah join Jesus on the mountain (4), though only Jesus is transfigured. Perhaps they represent the whole Old Testament revelation in the Law and the Prophets, but they have something else in common, too. With Moses, God's covenant with Israel had been made (see Ex 24:8), but Elijah saw clearly that Israel had broken the covenant (see 1 Kings 19:10). So God had promised a new covenant (see, for example, Jer 31:31-34, Joel 2:28-32, Ezek 36:24-27). And it is Jesus who will make this covenant reality, as John the Baptist had implied at the beginning of the Gospel (see 1:8) and as Jesus himself will make clear at the end (see 14:24). So it makes sense that Moses and Elijah are here.

Peter is in danger of seeing no real distinction between Moses, Elijah and Jesus, as his suggestion in verse 5 makes clear. So now, for the second time in the Gospel, God the Father speaks from heaven: "This is my Son, whom I love. Listen to him!" (7) At Jesus' baptism, the words were directed to Jesus (see 1:11); here at the transfiguration they are directed to Peter, James and John. The additional phrase "Listen to him!" recalls Moses' words about the Prophet-Messiah who would one day come (see Deut 18:15). In Jesus these words are being fulfilled.

On the way down the mountain the three disciples wonder what Jesus means by "rising from the dead" (9-10), but, probably because they have just seen Elijah, they ask a quite different question: "Why do the teachers of the law say that Elijah must come first?" (11) Jesus replies that the theologians are correct (see Mal 3:1; 4:5), but that Elijah has already come. The reference is to John the Baptist, who was not a reincarnation of Elijah (such an idea would contradict the Bible's teaching) but an Elijah-figure (see, for example, Luke 1:13-17), preparing the way for Jesus. With verse 13 we are reminded that the cost of discipleship was already a theme in Section Three (6:14-29).

Jesus drives out an evil spirit (9:14-29)

This is the last incident in Block A and Mark may have used his sandwiching technique to recount it. Verses 14-19 and verses 28 and 29 concern Jesus and the issue of the nine disciples' inability to heal the boy, while verses 20-27 show us the steps Jesus takes to work the miracle. The key theme in all three sections is faith. It is indispensable for all who want to follow Jesus.

In verses 14-19 Jesus, Peter, James and John return from their mountaintop experience to a suffering world (represented here by a father and his son, 17-18) and to the inability of the nine disciples. As the father explains, "I asked your disciples to drive out the spirit, but they could not" (18b).

Jesus explains this failure by lack of faith: "'O unbelieving generation,' Jesus replied, 'how long shall I stay with you?'" (19a)

In verses 20-27 Jesus talks to the father about his son's condition, and once again faith is the issue. In his anguish the man exclaims "But if you can do anything, take pity on us and help us" (22). Jesus' response is swift: "'If you can'? said Jesus. 'Everything is possible for him who believes'" (23). The father's response is desperate: "I do believe; help me overcome my unbelief!" (24) So Jesus heals the boy before too many spectators arrive (25-27).

The theme of faith is present, too, in verses 28 and 29. When the disciples ask Jesus to explain their inability to drive out the demon – despite the fact that he had given them authority to do just this (see 3:15 and 6:7, 13) – he replies: "This kind can come out only by prayer" (29).

Clearly there is a link between prayer and faith, and also between unbelief and powerlessness in spiritual things. The message is clear: the disciples need to learn not to rely on their gifts or even on the authority Jesus has given them, but on God. And this faith will inevitably lead to prayer.

The disciples' training did not stop at the end of Section Three. Here, at the beginning of Section Four, they are learning that Jesus the Messiah is the Son of Man and the divine Son of God, who must die and rise again; and that following him means giving up their own lives and relying not on their own ability but on his.

Block B (9:30-10:31)

a – The second prediction (9:30-32)

Mark makes it very clear what Jesus' overriding concern is in Block B: "Jesus did not want anyone to know where they were, because he was teaching his disciples" (30-31). This second prediction is less specific than the first (see 8:31), but it is enough to frighten the disciples: "But they did not understand what it meant and were afraid to ask him about it" (32).

Three mistakes disciples make (9:33-50)

b – "I am the greatest" (9:33-37)

The disciples are embarrassed when Jesus asks what they have been discussing; Mark tells us that "they had argued about who was the greatest" (34). Jesus uses this as a teaching opportunity and explains that servanthood is the hallmark of greatness (35). And Jesus uses a small child as a powerful visual aid: people who think themselves important have no time for "unimportant" children, but his disciples are to be different (36-37).

c – "We are the only ones" (9:38-41)

This second mistake originates with the disciple who was later, in his letters, to emphasize the importance of love: "'Teacher', said John, 'we saw a man driving out demons in your name and we told him to stop, because he was not one of us'" (38). "Do not stop him", says Jesus (39), "for whoever is not against us is for us" (40).

Jesus does not mean by this that everyone is right, whatever they believe; Mark tells us three times in four verses that the crucial thing is that everything should be done in Jesus' name (38, 39, 41), trusting in his authority and power and with an eye to his glory. But disciples must learn not to be proud and exclusive, but to be open to all those who follow Jesus.

We should also notice here that Jesus refers to future rewards for faithful disciples (41). The vision of future glory will give his followers courage to live for him in the present.

d – "Sin doesn't matter" (9:42-50)

This paragraph is about the seriousness of sin. Sometimes we cause others to sin, says Jesus (42), and sometimes we cause ourselves to sin (43-49). Jesus makes it clear here that to say "Sin doesn't matter" is to play with fire (almost literally, 43b, 48). His comments about cutting off a hand or a foot and gouging out an eye are deliberate exaggeration to emphasize the need for radical action against sin. The hand may refer to something I do, the foot to somewhere I go, and the eye to something I look at. But, whatever the situation, disciples must not take sin lightly.

As we have already seen, Mark has told us that the disciples had been arguing on the road (34). Now, in verse 50, Jesus says to them "Have salt in yourselves, and be at peace with each other." So these three mistakes belong together; and they are common enough today among Christians. If we compare ourselves with others ("I am the greatest"), try to exclude others who may be following Jesus as much as we are ("We are the only ones"), or ignore the seriousness of sin ("Sin doesn't matter"), we shall not be effective disciples of Jesus.

Three areas in which disciples should be different (10:1-27)

d' – Attitude to marriage (10:1-12)

In this paragraph the Pharisees come with a question about divorce (2). This is a trick question, but Jesus uses it as another teaching opportunity. The main emphasis, however, is not on divorce but on marriage: in verses 5-9 Jesus quotes from the first two chapters of Genesis to make clear the original purpose of God in inventing marriage. And he concludes: "Therefore what God has joined together, let man not separate" (9).

Although Jesus accepts that divorce may sometimes be permitted, he is making it clear that it always goes against God's original intention (5-6). And the disciples are listening (10-12): they must learn that Jesus' followers are not to marry thoughtlessly; for Christian disciples, marriage is for life.

c' – Attitude to children (10:13-16)

By means of Block B's mirror structure, Mark has linked Incidents c and c': in both cases disciples are trying to prevent others from serving or approaching Jesus. Here, parents are being rebuked (13) for bringing their children; presumably the disciples think their own conversation with Jesus is more important.

In the first century, children were seen as insignificant, and so Jesus' indignation must have surprised the disciples: "Let the little children come to me, and do not hinder them, for the kingdom of God belongs to such as these" (14).

There are two main lessons here: anyone who wants to enter the kingdom of God must receive it as a child receives a gift (15); and disciples must never think of children as unimportant.

b' – Attitude to possessions (10:17-27)

Mark now introduces us to a man who is determined to receive eternal life: he runs to Jesus and kneels down in front of him (17). Despite this show of humility, however, he is sure of his status, based on his goodness (18-20) and his possessions (21-22). This theme of status reminds us of the disciples in Incident b (9:33-37), arguing about who is the greatest.

But Jesus is drawn to this man: he "looked at him and loved him" (21). So, because of this, he tells him what he needs to hear: "Go, sell everything you have and give to the poor, and you will have treasure in heaven. Then come, follow me" (21).

This is not a condition for all would-be disciples. But everyone who wants to come into God's kingdom must give up everything which is more important to him than Jesus and the gospel (cf. 29). This is a huge challenge to those of us who have grown up in a culture so materialistic that we no longer notice the hold possessions have on us.

The cost of discipleship is sometimes too high: "At this the man's face fell. He went away sad, because he had great wealth" (22). And Jesus watches him go: he is not willing to accept second place in the lives of those who want to follow him.

This has all come as a frightening shock to the disciples. As we have already seen, status is important to them (see Incident b), and, as first-century Jews, they will have believed that rich people were closer to God than poor people: "The disciples were even more amazed, and said to each other, 'Who then can be saved?'" (26) Jesus' reply is designed to underline human inability to bring anyone into the kingdom, as well as God's ability: "For man this is impossible, but not with God; all things are possible with God" (27). It is significant that Jesus looks at his disciples again (cf. 8:33) before emphasizing human weakness.

It should be obvious that discipleship involves every aspect of life, and not just the activities we may like to think of as 'religious'. But here, in Incidents d', c' and b', Mark has highlighted three areas in which followers of Jesus must be radically different from the world around them: in their attitude to marriage, children and possessions. However, he ends Block B by recording Jesus making clear that disciples always gain much more than they lose.

a' – The rewards of discipleship (10:28-31)

These verses do not just apply to cross-cultural missionaries! Every disciple is called upon to embrace the kingdom priorities of Jesus and the gospel (29). It is fascinating to see the difference between the two lists in verses 29 and 30. The second list promises disciples persecution in this life and eternal life in the next, reflecting Jesus' death and resurrection in Incident a (see 9:31). A further difference is that the disciple gains "a hundred times as much" as he gives up (30).

But there is another difference which is often overlooked. The word "fathers" is missing from the second list in verse 30. The message is clear: while the disciple needs substitute brothers, sisters and mothers in the family of God, she needs no fathers – because through Jesus she has discovered the love of the heavenly Father.

So Block B is not only about the cost of discipleship. Jesus emphasizes its rewards too, both in this life and in the next. This vision of the future is what can motivate us to follow Jesus.

Mark ends Block B with Jesus' summary of the effects of the kingdom of God: "But many who are first will be last, and the last first" (31). As men and women renounce their sins (see Incidents b, c and d) and embrace a new lifestyle (see Incidents d', c' and b'), a divine reversal of human expectations takes place, so that the cost of discipleship is seen to be a small price to pay for life in the kingdom.

Block C (10:32-52)

The third prediction (10:32-34)

Jesus is leading the way up to Jerusalem (32), presumably because none of the others wants to go there: the disciples are astonished again and the others are frightened. The prediction which follows is the most detailed of the three, including a description of Jesus' suffering before his death at the hands of Gentiles (33-34). This time Mark does not tell us the reaction of the disciples; the impending crisis simply leads to a renewed concern for future status (35-45).

James and John's request (10:35-45)

The disciples have clearly not learned the lesson of 9:33-37. James and John want the best places in the kingdom of God (37); and when they hear about it, the other disciples are angry, not at the brothers' lack of humility but probably because James and John have managed to get their request in first (41). At least the two of them have grasped that that there is going to be a glorious kingdom and that the glory will belong to Jesus: "Let one of us sit at your right and the other at your left in your glory" (37). But there is still so much they have not understood about discipleship.

Following Jesus means three things. First, suffering – the cup (cf. 14:36) and the baptism are pictures of suffering which James and John are not going to want to share, despite their self-confidence (38-39). Secondly, following Jesus means submission – it is the Father who decides the issue of rewards and position in the kingdom of God (40). And, thirdly, discipleship means service, not lording it over others (42, cf. 1 Peter 5:3): "Whoever wants to become great among you must be your servant, and whoever wants to be first must be slave of all" (43-44).

The reason for this is Jesus' own example: "For even the Son of Man did not come to be served, but to serve, and to give his life as a ransom for many" (45). For the first time in the Gospel Jesus explains the *purpose* of his death. Verse 45 is a key statement for all who want to understand the Christian faith. Jesus' death, despite the plots of Jews and Gentiles (see 10:33), will be voluntary ("to *give* his life") and will be a sin-offering (the word "ransom" recalls the suffering servant of Isaiah 53:10) for the sake of others (see Is 53:12). Perhaps most important of all is the fact that his death was central to his purpose in coming into the world (45).

Mark does not tell us how the disciples respond to this statement –
perhaps because he wants to allow us, his readers, to respond for ourselves.

The healing of blind Bartimaeus (10:46-52)

Although he is blind, Bartimaeus can see something the crowd cannot
see: Jesus of Nazareth is the Son of David, the Messiah (47-48). So he
calls for help, and when the crowd tell him to be quiet, Mark tells us that
"he shouted all the more" (48). Jesus' question "What do you want me to
do for you?" (51) seems designed to reveal whether Bartimaeus has faith
or not; as with the healing of the demonized boy in Block A, faith is
essential (see 9:23-24) if the transforming power of Jesus is to be seen in
action.

After the healing, Bartimaeus follows Jesus along the road (52). Of
course Mark means a literal physical following here at the end of Block
C; but surely he means us to make a connection with Jesus' words near
the beginning of Block A: "If anyone would come after me, he must deny
himself and take up his cross and follow me" (8:34).

For at the end of Section Four we have a much clearer idea of the cost of
discipleship than we had at the beginning. Those who want to follow
Jesus must give up their self-centredness ("I am the greatest", "We are
the only ones", "Sin doesn't matter") and live with a new attitude to
marriage, children and possessions (9:33-10:27). But Mark wants us to
make no mistake: it is worth it (10:28-31), and he gives us Bartimaeus'
decision to become a disciple of Jesus as an example to follow.

There is a lesson for us all here. We need vision. The Christian hope of
future glory is what gives disciples the motivation they need to follow
Jesus now. Peter, James and John received that vision as they saw Jesus
transfigured as the glorious Son of God, and they never forgot it (See 2
Pet 1:16-18; 1 Pet 4:12-14; 5:1,10). So the experience of Bartimaeus is an
encouragement to us to pray "Lord, I want to see".

Learning the Gospel

I hope you will take time to learn Section Four – it is easy to learn and it
will help you re-discover Jesus and what it means to follow him. Begin
with Block B, with its clear structure of the second prediction, three
mistakes disciples make, three areas in which disciples should be
different, and the rewards of discipleship. Learn the headings; you can fill
in some of the details later.

Once you have grasped Block B, Blocks A and C will present no problem. And, as you take time to learn Section Four, I am sure you are doing what the first Christians did.

The Cost

A	First prediction 4
	The call to discipleship
	The transfiguration
	Jesus drives out an evil spirit

B	a Second prediction 1

	b "I am the greatest" 2
	c "We are the only ones"
	d "Sin doesn't matter"

	d' Attitude to marriage 3
	c' Attitude to children
	b' Attitude to possessions

	a' The rewards of discipleship 1

C	Third prediction 5
	James and John's request
	The healing of blind Bartimaeus

A+C:	following Jesus (8:34 / 10:52)
Logic B:	a, a': same pattern
	b, c, d: three mistakes disciples make
	d', c', b': three areas in which disciples should be different

Meeting the Lord

As you run through the section in your mind there will be a lot to talk to the Lord about. Worship Jesus as you see him transform lives in response to faith; pray about your own discipleship as you allow Jesus to teach you in Block B; and thank him for what it cost him to bring you forgiveness and reconciliation with God. And, above all else, ask him to open your eyes to see his glory.

As you do this – walking down the street or on your knees in your room – I pray that you will sense that Jesus is touching your life, showing you the next step in the adventure of discipleship, and allowing you to see his mercy, his authority and his love in a new way. You will be re-discovering Jesus.

When we pray as Bartimaeus prayed, we will experience what Bartimaeus experienced.

Section Five: The Judgment (Mark 11:1-13:37)

Mark has made it very clear in Section Four that Jesus knows exactly what will happen to him in Jerusalem (see, for example, 10:32-34). When he arrives it becomes clear that the religious leaders are still absolutely opposed to him. Their rejection of Jesus leads to his rejection of them as the leaders of God's people. This judgment is a major theme throughout Section Five.

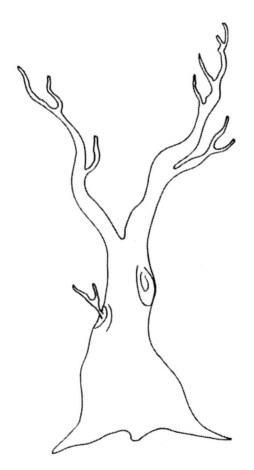

"In the morning, as they went along,
they saw the fig-tree withered from the roots."
(Mark 11:20)

Enjoying the View

Block A (11:1-25)

Jesus enters Jerusalem (1-11)
Jesus curses the fig-tree (12-14)
Jesus clears the temple (15-19)
Jesus teaches lessons about prayer from the fig-tree (20-25)

Block B (11:27-12:44)

a	11:27-33	The authority of Jesus questioned
b	12:1-12	The parable of the tenants
c	12:13-17	Paying taxes to Caesar
d	12:18-27	Marriage at the resurrection
d'	12:28-34	The greatest commandment
c'	12:35-37	A question about the Messiah
b'	12:38-40	Warning about the teachers of the law
a'	12:41-44	The widow's offering

Block C (13:1-37)

The destruction of the temple and the end of the world (1-37)

Mark makes clear for us the beginning and the end of Block B. In 11:27 Jesus comes into the temple for the last time, and in 13:1 he leaves the temple for the last time; and, once again, there are eight parts to this central section, linked together in a mirror structure (see below, *Unpacking the Content*).

The temple plays a key role in Section Five. In Block A Jesus comes to the temple, in Block B he teaches in the temple, and in Block C he teaches about the temple. But Blocks A and C have something in common more specific than the temple, namely the fig-tree. In Block A Jesus curses a fig-tree (11:14, 20-21); and in Block C he tells a short parable about a fig-tree (13:28). Mark has taken a great deal of trouble to structure the section clearly and memorably.

There is one very significant Mark sandwich here. In Block A, Jesus' assault on the abuse of the temple as he drives out the money changers and their colleagues is sandwiched between the cursing of the fig-tree and the disciples' discovery that the fig-tree is now withered (11:12-21).

Before we look at the text in more detail, please read the whole of Section Five for yourself. Imagine the scene, with its plotting, its emotion and its tensions, and ask the Lord to make it live in your imagination.

Unpacking the Content

Block A (11:1-25)

Jesus enters Jerusalem (11:1-11)

Mark tells us about Jesus arranging for a colt on which to ride into Jerusalem (1-7), but he does not tell us why this is significant. If the crowd's enthusiasm at Jesus' arrival is because they have understood that Jesus is fulfilling the messianic prophecy of Zechariah 9:9, it seems odd that Mark does not quote the verse. In any case, they are clearly welcoming him as a king: "Many people spread their cloaks on the road, while others spread branches they had cut in the fields" (8).

But the goal is not Jerusalem but specifically the temple (11). This is the first of three times Jesus comes to Israel's place of worship in this section (see also 15, 27). On this occasion Jesus does no more than observe what is happening: "He looked around at everything, but since it was already late, he went out to Bethany with the Twelve" (11). Mark is preparing us here for what will happen next.

Jesus curses the fig-tree (11:12-14)

The Mark sandwich which begins here links the fig-tree with the temple (12-21), so an observant reader might conclude that the fig-tree is a picture for Israel, a view which the Old Testament confirms (see, for example, Jer 8:13). So the cursing of the fig-tree is a visual message of judgment.

It is irrelevant to complain that Jesus' cursing of the fig-tree is unjustified. Although, as Mark tells us, "it was not the season for figs" (13), Jesus has every reason to expect early, edible buds, because the tree is in leaf. So he comes looking for fruit but finds none. This is the meaning of the next part of the sandwich.

Jesus clears the temple (11:15-19)

Now, as in verse 11, Jesus comes to the temple looking for fruit, the qualities which are to be expected in God's people. But he finds none. He walks in as if he owns the place, turning over the furniture and turning out the people buying and selling. And he explains his behaviour by accusing them of having made this "house of prayer" into "a den of robbers" (17).

The message is clear. Jesus comes to the focus of Jewish religion and should be able to see signs that God is known and worshipped here; he is more hungry for this spiritual fruit than he was for the early figs in verse 12. But there is nothing to be seen .— only people using the temple as a means of making money. The Jewish religion Jesus sees is all leaves and no fruit. No wonder he must act in judgment.

"The chief priests and the teachers of the law heard this", says Mark, "and began looking for a way to kill him" (18). This is the same decision the Pharisees and the Herodians first made in chapter 3, verse 6. But the reason is not so much anger at what Jesus has done in their temple, as fear of what his popularity among the people could lead to (18).

So Mark makes it clear that the Jewish leaders have made their decision about Jesus, and that he has made his decision about them. Judgment is a major theme in Block A.

Jesus teaches lessons about prayer from the fig-tree (11:20-25)

Mark completes his sandwich by telling us that, the following day, the disciples saw "the fig-tree withered from the roots" (20). Peter even finds it necessary to draw Jesus' attention to it! (21)

Jesus now seizes the opportunity to teach his disciples about prayer, the fruit which had been missing in the temple (17). The first condition for answered prayer is faith (22-24); the second is that the disciple's relationships with others are as they should be (25). Although Jesus here refers to the Father forgiving, it is worth remembering that Jesus' conflict with the Jewish leaders began back in Section One of the Gospel with his claim to be able to forgive sins himself (see 2:5, 10).

In Block A the lines have been clearly drawn. Jesus has come in judgment, and the Jewish leaders are determined to be rid of him. In Block B it will come to direct confrontation.

Block B (11:27-12:44)

a – The authority of Jesus questioned (11:27-33)

This is the first of eight incidents in the temple which will lead to Jesus' words of judgment in Block C. The Jewish leaders are on the attack: "'By what authority are you doing these things?' they asked. 'And who gave you authority to do this?'" (28) These two questions may be referring to Jesus' extraordinary behaviour in the temple (15-17), or perhaps to his earlier healings and exorcisms. But the issue is not what Jesus has done, but on whose authority he has done it.

Interestingly, Jesus ducks the question, either because he knows it does not reflect a genuine search for the truth, or because he realises that a direct answer would cause a riot – or worse. His own question, about the origin of John's baptism, puts his opponents on the spot: "If we say 'From heaven', he will ask, 'Then why didn't you believe him?' But if we say, 'From men...'" (31-32). Mark explains their problem at the end of verse 32: "They feared the people, for everyone held that John really was a prophet."

So the issue of authority has not been resolved. But the first shots have been fired. And it has become clear that the Jewish leaders, in their arrogance, are looking for an excuse to do away with Jesus.

b – The parable of the tenants (12:1-12)

Mark begins this paragraph by telling us that Jesus "began to speak to them in parables" (1). However, he records only one, which must therefore be the most important. It is not difficult to see why.

Like the fig-tree in Block A, the vineyard is an Old Testament picture of Israel. The details in verse 1 deliberately recall Isaiah 5:2: "He dug it up and cleaned it of stones and planted it with the choicest vines. He built a watchtower in it and cut out a winepress as well." Jesus' listeners must surely recognize the reference and understand, too, that the farmer-tenants are the spiritual leaders of Israel, who, through the centuries, have rejected God's prophets (2-7) and failed to give God the fruit they owe him.

Now Jesus reaches the climax of his story: "He had one left to send, a son, whom he loved. He sent him last of all, saying, 'They will respect my son'" (6). The description of the son recalls the Father's words about Jesus, both at his baptism (1:11) and at his transfiguration (9:7): "my Son, whom I love". How must Jesus be feeling as he says of the tenants: "They took him and killed him, and threw him out of the vineyard" (8)!

The owner's response in killing the tenants and giving the vineyard to others is followed by a quotation from Psalm 118 (from which the crowds have already quoted in 11:9): "The stone the builders rejected has become the capstone" (10). Once again, the message is clear: Jesus, the Son of the Father, is the stone which the leaders of Israel are rejecting and will kill; but God will make him the leader of a renewed people of God.

Once again, Jesus' opponents are wrong-footed (12). And he is provoking them more than ever.

c – Paying taxes to Caesar (12:13-17)

This time it is the turn of the Pharisees and the Herodians to try to trap Jesus, two groups – one religious, one secular – uniting at the end, as they had at the beginning (see 3:6), in order to destroy their common enemy. After a heavy-handed display of flattery, they ask their question: "Is it right to pay taxes to Caesar or not?" (14)

Jesus' answer "Give to Caesar what is Caesar's and to God what is God's" (17) leads to general amazement. Of course it does not answer all the questions about Church and State. But Mark underlines for us the fact that the question was not an honest one: "But Jesus knew their hypocrisy. 'Why are you trying to trap me?' he asked" (15; see also 13). The trick question is simply designed to provide an opportunity to do away with Jesus.

d – Marriage at the resurrection (12:18-27)

The Sadducees have been described as the liberal theologians of their day; they rejected the idea of life after death (18). Their funny story, designed to show how ridiculous the doctrine of resurrection is in practice (19-23), instead earns them a strong rebuke from Jesus: "Are you not in error because you do not know the Scriptures or the power of God?" (24)

Because the Sadducees only accepted the authority of the five books of Moses, Jesus goes on to prove the reality of life after death from the book of Exodus (26-27; Ex 3:6).

Again, the issue as it is presented by Jesus' opponents is not the real issue here. Mark's primary concern is not to teach us about the resurrection, but to show us that an influential group in first-century Judaism could be accused by Jesus of not knowing the Scriptures.

d' – The greatest commandment (12:28-34)

This paragraph introduces us to a leading Jew who is different. He is impressed by Jesus' debating skills and so asks a question: "Of all the commandments, which is the most important?" (28) In reply Jesus quotes Deuteronomy 6:4-5, about loving God, and Leviticus 19:18, about loving one's neighbour (29-31).

The teacher of the law is in complete agreement and his response is worth quoting in full: "'Well said, teacher', the man replied. 'You are right in saying that God is one and there is no other but him. To love him with all your heart, with all your understanding and with all your strength, and to love your neighbour as yourself is more important than all burnt offerings and sacrifices'" (32-33).

Jesus, in turn, is impressed by his answer: "You are not far from the kingdom of God" (34). Why is this the case? Surely it is because the teacher of the law knows the difference between leaves and fruit, between religious activities (important though they may be) and right relationships to God and other people.

With his mirror structure Mark is contrasting the teacher of the law in Incident d' with the Sadducees in Incident d. They do not know the Scriptures (24), but the teacher of the law certainly does: his reply in verses 32 and 33 betrays knowledge not only of the Deuteronomy passage Jesus has quoted, but also of passages like 1 Samuel 15:22, Hosea 6:6, and Micah 6:6-8. He knows the Jewish Scriptures – and believes them too. No wonder Mark writes: "And from then on no one dared ask him any more questions" (34).

c' – A question about the Messiah (12:35-37)

The mirror structure of Block B links this incident with Incident c (see 12:13-17). There Jesus is asked a question which is designed to be unanswerable (although Jesus manages to answer it!); here it is Jesus who asks an unanswerable question. If the teachers of the law call the Messiah the son of David, why is it that David refers to the Messiah in Psalm 110:1 as his Lord?

The answer, of course, is that the Messiah is, in one person, the human descendant of David and the divine Son of God. But Mark leaves us to work this out for ourselves. He tells us simply that "the large crowd listened to him with delight" (37).

b' – Warning about the teachers of the law (12:38-40)

Mark reminds us once again that he is not recording all of Jesus' teaching: "As he taught, Jesus said…" (38). Interestingly, there is a similar indicator at the beginning of Incident b (see 12:1), linked to this one by the mirror structure. But the two incidents have much more in common.

In verses 38-40 Jesus criticises the teachers of the law for their pride (38-39), their greed (40a) and their hypocrisy (40b). In other words, their long prayers are leaves without fruit. Jesus' judgment is devastating: "Such men will be punished most severely" (40c).

This is an obvious link with 12:9 in Incident b: "What then will the owner of the vineyard do? He will come and kill those tenants and give the vineyard to others". This is, surely, the severe punishment which awaits those of Israel's leaders who fail to give God the fruit which is his due.

a' – The widow's offering (12:41-44)

Jesus contrasts the generosity of the widow with the meanness of the rich: "I tell you the truth, this poor widow has put more into the treasury that all the others. They all gave out of their wealth; but she, out of her poverty, put in everything – all she has to live on" (43-44).

But there is another contrast too, as we compare Incidents a and a'. In 11:27-33 Jesus refuses to answer the questions posed by "the chief priests, the teachers of the law and the elders" (11:27). But here, in 12:41-44, Jesus praises one lonely widow. All they had to offer were two trick questions designed to destroy Jesus; what the widow has to offer are two small coins designed to glorify God.

Mark's Block B in Section Five is a devastating critique of much of the spiritual leadership in Israel. They have failed to get the better of Jesus, but their determination to end his life and their refusal to give God the fruit of lives dedicated to him mean that God's judgment must surely come. This will be a major theme in Block C.

Block C (13:1-37)

The destruction of the temple and the end of the world (13:1-37)

In verse 1 Mark tells us that Jesus leaves the temple. Although this is a physical description, it is surely more than that: the conflict with Israel's leaders means that Jesus will never return to the temple – indeed he predicts its destruction in verse 2.

The question which Peter, James, John and Andrew ask in verse 4 is crucial: "Tell us, when will these things happen? And what will be the sign that they are about to be fulfilled?" The rest of Block C is Jesus' answer to the question.

This is the most difficult part of Mark's Gospel to interpret; I recommend the commentaries to those who want to study it in detail. Two things, however, are clear: Jesus predicts both the destruction of the temple (which was to happen in AD 70) and his own return to this world in glory at the end of the age. What causes the difficulty is that it is not always clear at any given point in the chapter to which of the two events Jesus is referring. It is as if Jesus is looking at God's judgment in history through a telescope, when the slightest twist of the wrist means that this judgment is no longer being seen in the context of the temple's destruction but in the context of his own return.

Verses 1-4, as we have already seen, form an introduction, with Jesus' shocking prediction of the events of AD 70 and the disciples' private question as to when all this will happen.

Verses 5-13 seem to focus mainly (but not exclusively) on the troubles leading up to the destruction of the temple. There will be false prophets (5-6), claiming to be the Messiah or to be teaching with his authority; there will be suffering (7-8), as wars and natural disasters make it essential to be alert; and there will be persecution (9-13), as Gentiles and Jews attack Jesus' disciples (9), and as families are torn apart by different attitudes to Jesus (12).

Verses 14-23 seem to take us to the moment of crisis. The expression "the abomination that causes desolation" (14) is taken from the book of Daniel in the Old Testament (see, for example 9:27; 11:31; 12:11). When hundreds of Jews were killed in the temple in the years leading up to AD 70, Christians saw this as a fulfilment of Mark 13:14. But it is also possible to see a later fulfilment in the appearance of an Antichrist, predicted by the Apostle Paul in 2 Thessalonians 2:3-4. Perhaps verses 14-23 should be read with the focus of the telescope constantly shifting to and fro.

Verses 24-27, on the other hand, seem to be focused firmly on the return of Jesus. They describe the end of the world (24-25), and then the arrival of the King: "At that time men will see the Son of Man coming in clouds with great power and glory" (26). And Jesus takes the opportunity to emphasize that God's children will be safe (27).

Verses 28-31 turn the telescope back to the events of AD 70. The fig tree of verse 28 must not refer to Israel bursting into life; it may simply be a parable encouraging watchfulness (as well as a memory marker linking Block C with Block A). If this interpretation is correct, Jesus is teaching here that the destruction of the temple will come soon: "I tell you the truth, this generation will certainly not pass away until all these things have happened" (30)[*]. And, even though we are sometimes unsure of Jesus' meaning, his authority is not in doubt: "Heaven and earth will pass away, but my words will never pass away" (31).

---

[*] The expression "these things" in Block C seems to refer to the destruction of the temple, while the expression "those days" refers to the return of Christ. See the commentaries for details.

Finally, **verses 32-37** form a conclusion to Jesus' teaching. Parts of this paragraph could be seen as advice for disciples living before the destruction of the temple, but the main focus is certainly Jesus' own return. Immediately after emphasizing his authority (31), Jesus teaches his ignorance of the timing of this last great event in human history: "No one knows about that day or hour, not even the angels in heaven, nor the Son, but only the Father" (32).

In the light of this, Christian disciples should be wary of dogmatism about the details and the timing of the second coming of Jesus. Block C is not here to provide fuel for wild speculation, but instead to encourage us to watch (5, 9, 23, 33, 36 and 37).

So Section Five ends with a short parable to encourage us to stay awake in our discipleship (34-36). Just as the crowds welcomed Jesus at the beginning of the section, so we need to be ready and waiting to welcome him when the end comes. So the message of Block C is summed up in its last word, as Jesus says to us: "Watch!" (37)

In Section One of the Gospel we witnessed the confrontation between the old wineskins of empty religion and the new wine which Jesus brings. There, in the second half of Block B, the Jewish leaders were accusing him (see 2:7, 16, 18, 24); here, in Section Five, it is Jesus who is accusing them. And his main complaint is their lack of fruit (11:12-13, 15-17; 12:2, 15, 24, 38-40): they are not living as the people of God should be living. And so, explaining the parable of 12:1-8, Jesus answers his own question: "What then will the owner of the vineyard do? He will come and kill those tenants and give the vineyard to others" (9).

This does not mean that God has stopped loving the Jews; indeed the New Testament makes it clear that God has plans of future blessing for his ancient people (see Ro 11:25-36).

But we have already seen that Jesus has been calling a new people of God into existence (see comments on 1:13, 14-20; 3:13-14, 31-35). This is the Church, which consists of all people – whether Jews or Gentiles – who fulfil the kingdom conditions of repentance and faith (see 1:15).

But this fact should not make Christians complacent. Just as Jesus came to Israel at his first coming to look for fruit (see 11:13; 12:1-8), so he will come to the new Israel, the Church, at his second coming (see 13:34-35).

Jesus has the right to see fruit in the lives of those who follow him.

Learning the Gospel

Start, as always, with Block B. There is no pattern here to make this particularly easy, but if you have already learnt the first four sections of the Gospel, this should present you with no real problems. Learn Incidents a, b, c and d before going on to Incidents d', c', b' and a'. The mirror links will certainly help. Fill in the details as you run through the block in your mind, and the order of events will become more and more clear.

Block A looks long, but the sandwich after Jesus' arrival in Jerusalem makes it easy to remember. When you come to Block C, don't try to learn this in any kind of detail. If you just learn the heading "The destruction of the temple and the end of the world" you should already be able to add a few details to each of these two main themes.

If you remember that the title of Section Five is "The Judgment", it will remind you that in this section the leaders of Israel are rejecting Jesus and that he is rejecting them. These are serious issues but Mark wants us to think them through.

The Judgment

A	Jesus enters Jerusalem 3
	Jesus curses the fig-tree
	Jesus clears the temple
	Jesus teaches lessons about prayer from the fig-tree

B	a The authority of Jesus questioned 1
	b The parable of the tenants
	c Paying taxes to Caesar
	d Marriage at the resurrection

	d' The greatest commandment 2
	c' A question about the Messiah
	b' Warning about the teachers of the law
	a' The widow's offering

C	The destruction of the temple and the end 4
	of the world

A+C: fig-tree (11:13 / 13:28)

Logic B: Jesus goes into the temple for the last time
              (11:27)
              Jesus leaves the temple for the last time
              (13:1)

Meeting the Lord

I hope you will take time to talk the section through with the Lord. He wants to hear your ideas and questions about each part. Run through the section trying to imagine Jesus' feelings as the story unfolds; next time through, stop after each paragraph and worship him. And pray that the fruit of knowing Jesus will become more and more visible in your life.

I pray that you will re-discover Jesus as you spend time with him in Section Five. He is waiting to meet you.

Section Six: The Love (Mark 14:1-16:8)

The whole Gospel has been leading up to this section: here, we are going to experience the climax of the story Mark has to tell. In Section Six we will meet betrayal, hatred, fear and despair, but most of all we will see love. We will see the depth of Jesus' love at the cross and its triumph at the empty tomb. This is holy ground, and it should move us to stand here.

"And they crucified him." (Mark 15:24a)

Enjoying the View

Block A (14:1-11)

>   Plans against Jesus (1-2)
>   The anointing at Bethany (3-9)
>   Plans against Jesus (10-11)

Block B (14:12-15:39)

a	14: 12-26	The last supper
b	14: 27-31	Jesus predicts Peter's denial
c	14: 32-42	Gethsemane
d	14: 43-52	Jesus arrested
d'	14: 53-65	Before the Jewish Council
c'	14: 66-72	Peter denies Jesus
b'	15: 1-15	Jesus before Pilate
a'	15: 16-39	The crucifixion

Block C (15:40-16:8)

>   The women at the cross (15:40-41)
>   The burial of Jesus (15:42-47)
>   The resurrection (16:1-8)

There are two Mark sandwiches in Section Six. In Block A, the anointing at Bethany is sandwiched between the plans of Jesus' enemies to kill him, so there is a pattern of hate-love-hate. In Block C, the burial of Jesus is sandwiched between two mentions of the women who were his disciples (see 15:40-41, 47). Like all the others, Section Six has been structured very carefully.

What Block A and Block C have in common is the theme of anointing. In Block A Jesus is anointed by the woman at Bethany, and he explains its significance: "She poured perfume on my body beforehand to prepare for my burial" (14:8). And in Block C Mark tells us what happened early on Sunday morning: "When the Sabbath was over, Mary Magdalene, Mary the mother of James, and Salome bought spices so that they might go to anoint Jesus' body" (16:1). So Blocks A and C give us two anointings, the second of which does not take place. The resurrection makes it unnecessary.

The incidents in Block B are grouped in pairs. After the last supper Jesus predicts that Peter will deny him (Incidents a and b); Jesus prays in Gethsemane and is then arrested there (Incidents c and d); while Jesus is being cross-examined by the high priest, Peter is denying his master in the courtyard below (Incidents d' and c'); and Jesus' trial before the Roman governor leads to his crucifixion by Roman soldiers (Incidents b' and a').

Please take time to read through Section Six at one sitting. In Block A you will see the love of an unnamed woman for Jesus; in Block C you will see the love of Joseph for Jesus; and in Block B you will see Jesus' love for you. Try to imagine the scene and to think yourself into the sandals of all those who have anything to do with Jesus. As you read, you may find yourself stopping to worship.

Unpacking the Content

Block A (14:1-11)

Plans against Jesus (14:1-2)

This is the beginning of a Mark sandwich (1-11), which contrasts the hatred of Jewish leaders (1-2, 10-11) with the love of one woman (3-9). While most people are in Jerusalem to celebrate Passover to thank God for rescuing Israel from slavery in Egypt, "the chief priests and teachers of the law were looking for some sly way to arrest Jesus and kill him" (1).

The anointing at Bethany (14:3-9)

The woman here is almost certainly Mary (cf. John 12:1-11), but Mark decides not to tell us her name. He wants us to focus not on her identity but on her love.

The perfume she pours over Jesus is "very expensive" (3) and "could have been sold for more than a year's wages" (5). This extravagance earns her the indignant criticism of some of the people there. Mark writes: "And they rebuked her harshly" (5).

But Jesus springs to her defence. He describes her action as beautiful (6) and as right: "The poor you will always have with you, and you can help them any time you want. But you will not always have me" (7). Jesus is not saying that the poor are unimportant, but that, at this precise moment, anointing him was the right thing to do. More than that: it was prophetic (8). Usually you anoint a body after its owner has died! But somehow this woman senses that Jesus is soon to die, and that moves her to this prophetic act of love.

In verse 9 Jesus adds that this anointing is unforgettable: "I tell you the truth, wherever the gospel is preached throughout the world, what she has done will also be told, in memory of her." Jesus clearly expects that the good news about him will be talked about all over the world, but he is so impressed by this woman's love that he promises that her extravagance will never be forgotten. It is almost as if Jesus is guaranteeing that this will be part of the New Testament!

It is not hard to see why this extravagant act of love is so important to Jesus. He has come to Jerusalem to perform the most extravagant act of love the world will ever see: he will die on the cross for our sins. And, surrounded as he is by the hatred of the leaders and the incomprehension of his friends, this one woman's love must have meant so much to him.

Plans against Jesus (14:10-11)

Jesus' reaction to the anointing seems to have been the last straw for Judas, who goes to the chief priests with an offer they cannot refuse (10). The contrast between the hatred at the beginning and the end of Block A and the love in between could not be greater. The scene is set for the events of Block B.

Block B (14:12-15:39)

a – The last supper (14:12-26)

Mark's mirror structure in Block B links this incident with the cruci-fixion, and the connection is not hard to find. Incident a explains Incident a'. The events of the last supper explain the meaning of Jesus' death.

Jesus clearly sees this last meal with his friends as being very important: he has gone to great lengths to make the necessary practical arrangements (13-16). The reason is that the disciples will learn how Israel's leaders are going to be able to kill him – he will be betrayed by one of their group (18-21). But, even more importantly, Jesus explains the meaning of his death, by using the bread and wine which were part of every Passover meal.

As the disciples drink the wine, Jesus says: "This is my blood of the covenant, which is poured out for many" (24). The words "for many" remind us of Jesus' words at the end of Section Four, when he says that he has come "to give his life as a ransom for many" (10:45). But the mention of the covenant takes us back much further, to the Old Testament promises that God would one day make a new covenant in which men and women would find forgiveness in a relationship with God (see Jer 31:31-34) through the presence of the Holy Spirit (see Ezek 36:26-27). John the Baptist had referred to this when he was preaching about Jesus (see 1:8), and now Jesus is saying that it is his death which will make this new covenant possible. He will die to make it possible for us to know God.

In verse 25 Jesus refers to the messianic banquet in heaven one day (see on 6:34-44); that, too, is being made possible by his death. But it is not only Jesus who explains the meaning of the cross at the last supper. Mark explains it too, by the way he introduces it. It was the time, he says, "when it was customary to sacrifice the Passover lamb" (12). Jesus' death will be a sacrifice. Mark has understood this and he wants us to understand it too.

b – Jesus predicts Peter's denial (14:27-31)

First, Jesus predicts that all the disciples will desert him, and he quotes from the Old Testament to prove it: "'I will strike the shepherd, and the sheep will be scattered'" (27). The interesting thing about the quotation from Zechariah 13:7 is that God is speaking: the death of Jesus is not only the result of the actions of Jews or Romans – it is something God himself is doing (cf. Isaiah 53:10).

This desertion will not be forever, as verse 28 makes clear with its reference to the resurrection. But Peter, typically self-confident, is sure that he will never disown Jesus, although he does not rule out the possibility that the other disciples will (29), which is tantamount to saying "I am the greatest" (see 9:33-37). And Jesus' prediction that Peter will deny him three times (30) causes Peter to contradict his Lord as he has before: "But Peter insisted emphatically, 'Even if I have to die with you, I will never disown you'" (31, cf. 8:32). Mark adds: "And all the others said the same" (31b).

c – Gethsemane (14:32-42)

Mark wants us to see Jesus' anguish as he thinks of the cross: "He began to be deeply distressed and troubled" (33). And he is not afraid to communicate this to Peter, James and John, his closest friends: "My soul is overwhelmed with sorrow to the point of death,' he said to them. 'Stay here and keep watch'" (34). And yet, three times, they fall asleep (37, 40, 41). And so Jesus warns them: "Watch and pray so that you will not fall into temptation" (38). None of them is going to heed the warning.

But Mark's emphasis here is on Jesus' prayer: "'Abba, Father', he said, 'everything is possible for you. Take this cup from me. Yet not what I will, but what you will'" (36). Jesus uses the most intimate Aramaic word for 'father', and he asks that he might not have to go to the cross. This is not because of the physical pain but because of the spiritual cost: as the Passover lamb (see 12), Jesus will take the divine judgment on to himself which others deserve. And three times the answer is No; there is no other way for sinners to be saved. And so, at the end of this paragraph Jesus goes to meet his betrayer (41-42). He has made his decision.

d – Jesus arrested (14:43-52)

Mark wants to emphasize Jesus' loneliness. Judas is "one of the Twelve" (43) and he arrives in Gethsemane with an armed crowd and with a kiss of betrayal (45). As Jesus is arrested one of the disciples resorts to violence in order to engineer an escape (45, cf. Jn 18:10). But Jesus knows that "the Scriptures must be fulfilled" (49).

And it is at this moment that the loneliness Jesus must have felt as he prayed becomes even more intense. Mark tells us simply: "Then everyone deserted him and fled" (50). And these are not his enemies – they are his best friends.

Only Mark tells us of another young man who ran away (51-52). It is possible that it was Mark himself who had slipped into the garden, drawn by the noise of the crowd in the darkness. We do not know, but if it was Mark, this is not the last time he would run away (cf. Acts 13:13). And, whether this is Mark or not, Jesus is now alone.

d' – Before the Jewish Council (14:53-65)

There is an extra sandwich which starts here in verse 53 and ends in verse 72. By mentioning Peter before he recounts Jesus' cross-examination before the Council, Mark makes clear that incidents d' and c' are happening at the same time: while Jesus is being interrogated by his enemies, his friend is denying all knowledge of him.

With his mirror structure Mark draws our attention to the contrast between Jesus' courage here in Incident d' and the disciples' cowardice in running away at the arrest (Incident d). We are left in no doubt that Jesus is innocent, because even the dishonest witnesses contradict each other (55-59); the evidence against him does not stand up.

When the high priest begins to interrogate him, Jesus does not defend himself but remains silent (60-61a). But when it comes to a direct question about his identity, silence is out of the question (61b-62). Jesus' courage here is astonishing: he must know that his claim to be the Messiah and the Son of God can only lead to his condemnation. His love for his Father and his love for sinners mean that he is determined to go to the cross.

c' – Peter denies Jesus (14:66-72)

Mark links this incident with the events in Gethsemane in Incident c. There, Jesus had prayed three times; here, Peter denies him three times. But there is another link too. In Gethsemane Jesus had given all his disciples a warning: "Watch and pray so that you will not fall into temptation" (38).

Now Mark shows us that Peter has not taken the warning to heart. While Jesus has been standing alone before the Sanhedrin, he has been sitting in the courtyard outside (54, 67). His claim to have no connection with Jesus is the proof that he has not been watching and praying. So Peter's denial fulfils not only verse 30 but also verse 38. Mark surely wants us to make the connection and to take steps ourselves so that temptation will not get the better of us the way it did of Peter.

b' – Jesus before Pilate (15:1-15)

The early morning meeting of the Jewish Council (1) is necessary because Jewish law did not allow it to meet at night. Before Pilate, Jesus once again refuses to defend himself (4-5), but once again is open about his identity (2).

Mark tells us that Pilate sees through the chief priests: he offers to release Jesus "knowing it was out of envy that the chief priests had handed Jesus over to him" (10). But the pressure of the crowd makes Pilate's attempt to do the right thing short-lived: "Wanting to satisfy the crowd, Pilate released Barabbas to them. He had Jesus flogged, and handed him over to be crucified" (15).

The mirror link with Incident b underlines Jesus' loneliness again. Jesus had predicted that his friends would desert him (see 14:27-31); now the crowds, some of whom had welcomed him in a spectacular way into Jerusalem on Palm Sunday (see 11:1-11), are shouting "Crucify him!" (13-14).

Mark may want us to learn another lesson here. He has already made it clear that Jesus is innocent, and Pilate agrees with this verdict (14a). But Mark goes out of his way to tell us that Barabbas, set free by Pilate instead of Jesus, is guilty as charged: "A man called Barabbas was in prison with the insurrectionists who had committed murder in the uprising" (7). In other words, the condemnation of an innocent man means the release of a guilty one. For us this is the good news of the cross.

a' – The crucifixion (15:16-39)

This final part of Block B is the climax to which Mark has been bringing us since Section One of his Gospel (see 2:20; 3:6). In Section Four Jesus has predicted his own death (see 8:31; 9:31; 10:33-34); but there has been little explanation until the last supper in Section Six (14:12-26, but see 10:45). Here, the mirror structure linking Incidents a and a' teaches us the meaning of the crucifixion.

Mark underlines for us the depth of Jesus' suffering. His battering at the hands of the soldiers in verses 16-20 and his flogging before it (15) make him physically incapable of carrying his own cross (21). When Mark writes "They brought Jesus to the place called Golgotha" (22) he uses a very physical word: they have almost to drag him there, not because he does not want to go but because he is not able. In verse 23 he refuses an anaesthetic – Jesus is determined to do nothing to lessen his suffering for us.

"And they crucified him" (24). Mark gives us no physical description of the sufferings involved, perhaps because he wants us to focus on something else. His three references to the time (25, 33, 34) may help us to see things as Mark wants us to see them.

First, from 9 o'clock, there are three hours of mockery (25-32). Although there are three men being crucified (27), this mockery is directed at Jesus: "Those who passed by hurled their insults at *him...*" (29). The religious leaders are enjoying the spectacle (31-32), and even the robbers crucified next to Jesus summon up the energy to jeer at him (32b). Mark surely wants us to see the irony in what the chief priests say, though it is certainly lost on them: "'He saved others', they said, 'but he can't save himself!'" (32b) The truth, of course, is somewhat different: it was in order to save others that he did not save himself.

Secondly, from midday, there are three hours of darkness (33). This is not an eclipse of the sun, which could never take place at Passover. No, this is an intervention by God, creating an unnatural darkness in the creation as the Creator dies (see John 1:3; Col 1:16).

And thirdly, at 3 o'clock, Jesus cries out "'Eloi, Eloi, lama sabachthani?'" (34), which Mark translates for us: "My God, my God, why have you forsaken me?" We are given no answer to the question, but there is only one thing in the universe which can separate a man or woman from God, and that is human sin. But Mark, as we have already seen, has made it clear that Jesus is innocent; so surely he wants us to see now that the sin separating Jesus from his Father is not his but ours. An innocent man is dying in the place of guilty sinners.

This explanation of the cross is confirmed by Mark's account of what happens when Jesus dies: "The curtain of the temple was torn in two from top to bottom" (38). The curtain before the Holy of Holies kept the worshippers in the temple out of the presence of God: their sin made access to his holiness impossible. But now the curtain has gone, because Jesus has died. With the death of Jesus and the tearing of the curtain, God is saying to anyone who will listen, "The price has been paid; you can come in now."

Verse 39 tells us about one man's response to the crucifixion: "And when the centurion, who stood there in front of Jesus, heard his cry and saw how he died, he said, 'Surely this man was the Son of God!'" This Roman soldier is the first person in Mark's Gospel to understand this about Jesus. Way back in Section One the Father had announced Jesus' identity at his baptism (see 1:11) and the forces of evil had recognised him too (see 1:34; 3:11). But now, in Section Six, for the first time, a human being calls Jesus the Son of God. And the extraordinary thing is that he is a Gentile.

Do you remember how Mark begins his introduction to the Gospel? "The beginning of the gospel about Jesus Christ, the Son of God" (1:1). At the end of Section Three the first human being saw in Jesus the Christ, the Messiah: "Peter answered, 'You are the Christ'" (8:29). And now, near the end of Section Six, a Roman centurion says "Surely this man was the Son of God!" (15:39)

We do not know how much he understood or what he meant by these words. But Mark wants us to recognize that the man on the cross is not just a tragic figure suffering an unjust death; he is the eternal Son of God, dying for the sins of the world. Mark wants us to worship the Christ, the Son of God.

Block C (15:40-16:8)

The women at the cross (15:40-41)

There is another Mark sandwich here. Verses 42-46 describe Jesus' burial, while on either side of it Mark mentions the women (40-41; 47). The women are more faithful than the men. The apostles have deserted Jesus, but the women are still there, watching as he dies.

The burial of Jesus (15:42-47)

Mark tells us about Joseph of Arimathea, a member of the Jewish Council and, until this moment, a secret disciple: he "was himself waiting for the kingdom of God" (43). Now he finds the courage to ask Pilate for Jesus' body: at the end of the paragraph he has come out as a follower of Jesus. Mark may be encouraging his readers to do the same.

The sandwich ends with verse 47, as two of the women note the location of the tomb. The stage is set for the great event of Sunday morning.

The resurrection (16:1-8)

Three of the women go to the tomb in order to anoint Jesus' body, but the spices they have bought for the purpose (see 1) will not be used today. In Block A of this section we saw that Jesus' body has already been anointed for burial (see 14:3-9, especially 8).

The open tomb and the appearance of the angel (whom Mark describes as looking like a young man, 5) fill them with fear. Imagine their feelings as he gives them the astonishing news that Jesus has risen from the dead. Before they can begin to take this in, the women are given a job to do: "But go, tell his disciples and Peter, 'He is going ahead of you into Galilee. There you will see him, just as he told you'" (7). It is very unlikely that the disciples had understood this message when they first heard it (see 14:28), so now they are to hear it again.

And there is a special message for Peter in the words of the angel. If the two words "and Peter" had not been there in verse 7, he might well have concluded that Jesus wanted nothing more to do with him: his arrogant self-confidence (see 14:29-31) and cowardly denial (see 14:66-72) had surely disqualified him for ever from being a disciple of Jesus. But the risen Jesus clearly sees things differently! He wants to forgive Peter and use him to tell others the good news about forgiveness.

But the message will not be passed on immediately. The last verse of Section Six is chapter 16, verse 8: "Trembling and bewildered, the women went out and fled from the tomb. They said nothing to anyone, because they were afraid." This temporary disobedience is perhaps understandable, but this is nevertheless a failure to obey the angel's message.

But we, the readers of the Gospel, are not afraid. We know that the resurrection is a fact of history, the confirmation that the message of the cross is true. At the end of Section Six the women are full of question marks, while the angel's certainty is an exclamation mark: "He is risen!" (6) Mark wants us to make the journey from doubt to faith, to allow Jesus' love for us to transform us.

Learning the Gospel

Please take time to learn Section Six; I am sure that the early Christians did.

Begin, once again, with Block B. Remember that the first incident (a) explains the last (a'): the last supper gives us the meaning of the crucifixion. Remember, too, that the events in Block B are in pairs: the last supper leads into Jesus' prediction of Peter's denial; his prayer in Gethsemane is followed by his arrest there; while Jesus is being interrogated before the Jewish Council Peter is denying his Lord in the courtyard outside; and the Roman governor hands Jesus over to be crucified by Roman soldiers.

Once you have got the main events of Block B in your mind, move on to Blocks A and C. Block A is a love-hate-love sandwich, making it easy to learn. Block C begins with another sandwich (women/burial/women); and it should not be difficult to remember that the section ends with the resurrection!

The Love

| A | Plans against Jesus
The anointing at Bethany
Plans against Jesus | 5 |

| B | a The last supper
b Jesus predicts Peter's denial | 1 |

| | c Gethsemane
d Jesus arrested | 2 |

| | d' Before the Jewish Council
c' Peter denies Jesus | 3 |

| | b' Jesus before Pilate
a' The crucifixion | 4 |

| C | The women at the cross
The burial of Jesus
The resurrection | 6 |

A+C: oil/anointing (14:8 / 16:1)

Logic B: grouped in pairs

Meeting the Lord

As you move through the events of Section Six in your mind, take time to stop, to thank Jesus for his love at every step of the way, and to worship him. Ask him to make these events real to you; ask him to touch your heart with his love; ask him to change your life. You may want to pray that you will not be like Peter, but like the woman who anoints Jesus in Block A.

For the recognition of his love for us should lead to a deepening of our love for him. I pray that that will be your experience as you open yourself up to the risen Jesus.

Mark's Conclusion (Mark 16:9-20)

Or is it? Most theologians think that verses 9-20 are a later addition to the Gospel: either the original ending got lost or Mark stopped writing at verse 8. They may be right. Whatever the truth of the matter, this conclusion was certainly written very early.

Enjoying the View

a   The appearances of the risen Lord (9-14)
b   The message of the sending Lord (15-18)
c   The disciples of the ascended Lord (19-20)

Although this conclusion to the Gospel may not be by Mark, it does fit the introduction rather well. In 1:1-8 and in 16:9-20 a major theme is witnesses telling the good news about Jesus. However, in the introduction they *come* to tell the good news, while in the conclusion they *go* to tell the good news. In the introduction the witnesses are Mark, the Old Testament prophets and John the Baptist; in the conclusion the witnesses are some disciples, the eleven apostles – and us, who believe their message.

Unpacking the Content

a – The appearances of the risen Lord (16:9-14)

There are two major elements here. First, Jesus is alive. He appears to Mary Magdalene (9-11, cf Jn 20:10-18), to two disciples walking in the country (12-13, cf Lk 24:13-32), and then to the eleven apostles (14, cf. Jn 20:26-29).

The second major element is that the apostles didn't believe it (11, 13). And Jesus rebukes them for this unbelief in verse 14.

b – The message of the sending Lord (16:15-18)

Now Jesus sends the apostles into the whole world to preach the good news (15, cf 1:1, 15; Mt 28:19). The message is that faith is indispensable in order to be saved (16), and the second half of the verse makes it clear that baptism is not a condition for salvation.

Then Jesus promises to confirm the message by miracles, although the promise is not necessarily that every individual will do these things, but the Church as a whole (16-18).

c – The disciples of the ascended Lord (16:19-20)

Verse 19 tells us that Jesus ascended into heaven and is now sitting in the place of authority – at the Father's right hand.

And verse 20 shows us that the apostles' unbelief has turned to faith. They do what their Lord has commanded them to do and he keeps his promise to confirm their message.

Learning the Gospel

Just learn the three headings, which are in a logical order.

Meeting the Lord

Run through verses 9-20 in your mind. Worship the risen Lord and ask him to increase your faith; listen to the sending Lord who is also sending you into the world to share the good news; and obey the ascended Lord by deciding to go wherever he sends you.

And you will continue to re-discover Jesus and get to know him better.

My Conclusion: The Experiment goes on

I hope you have taken time on the way through *The Mark Experiment* to learn the structure of the Gospel. If you have, then you have heard Jesus announcing the message of the kingdom of God; you have watched him demonstrating its reality by his parables and miracles; you have seen him training his disciples and helping them to recognize him as the Messiah; you have heard him teaching them what discipleship means and explaining that he will suffer, die and rise again; you have watched him responding to the attacks of the religious leaders and warning them of God's coming judgment in the destruction of their temple; and you have seen him dying on the cross as the Saviour of the world and appearing alive to his disciples to send them out into the world with the good news of the Gospel. I hope you have begun to re-discover Jesus.

But that process doesn't need to stop because you have reached the end of this book. I want to suggest a few ways in which you can use Mark's Gospel to get to know Jesus better.

1. Using Mark's Gospel for worship and prayer

Take one section of Mark. As you begin to run through it in your mind (without your Bible), don't just remember the events in order; instead, talk to Jesus about what he is saying and doing. Take time to enjoy being in his presence: worship him for his power and love, and pray for yourself as you think through the section's events.

You can do this at home in your room, or while you are sitting in the bus. You might decide to use Section One in this way for a week; the following week you could move on to Section Two.

2. Using Mark's Gospel to help you pray for others

Sometimes you feel you want to pray for a friend or a member of your family, but you are not sure how to pray. Why not take one section of the Gospel and pray through it, praying the whole time for this special person?

With some incidents you will be praying that she will recognise more and more who Jesus is and why he came; sometimes you will be praying that she will not make the mistakes the disciples make; sometimes you will pray that she will grow in faith and love. The Gospel can help you pray for others, whether these people are already Christians or not.

3. Using Mark's Gospel for a Mark walk

Go for a walk (without a Bible) with a friend who has learnt the structure of Mark. Take turns to tell each other the incidents as if the other person had never read the Gospel; if you can't remember what comes next or you forget some of the details, your friend can help you. You may decide to do half the Gospel or the whole Gospel, depending on how much time you have available, or on how many sections you have learnt.

The Mark Walk works well with a group too. But if there are more than four or five of you, you may have trouble hearing what is being said. The first time I went on a Mark Walk, there were fifteen of us, walking through the Austrian Alps. Every five minutes or so we stopped, and stood in a circle as one of us told the next incident. The rest of us were there to help. We were out for two and a half hours and during that time we told one another the whole Gospel from start to finish. And we re-discovered Jesus.

4. Using Mark's Gospel in a teaching programme

Your youth group or student group might decide to use the structure of Mark in its term programme. You could take one section a week – or one section a month – and re-discover Jesus through a talk or through small group discussion. Some of the group might decide to learn the structure of the Gospel for themselves, so that they can get to know Jesus better.

This would work well, too, in a church's Sunday teaching programme. The church leadership might decide on a sermon series in Mark's Gospel. The first sermon could deal with Mark's Introduction (1:1-8) and make the congregation excited to get to know Jesus better. Then you could have two or three sermons on each section.

5. Using Mark's Gospel in a house-group

It is possible to study the whole of the Gospel – and to learn it too – in a house-group context. There is a suggested series outline in Appendix 2.

6. Using Mark's Gospel for a drama event

The structure of Mark outlined in this book makes it possible to present the whole of the Gospel in dramatic form. One version of this involves between 40 and 120 people dividing into six groups, which then each present one section of the Gospel. In the other version a team of 15 people from a church or student group present the whole Gospel. There are some details of this in Appendix 1, and more on the Mark Experiment website – http://www.themarkexperiment.com.

I have given you six ideas about how to use Mark's Gospel to help you to get to know Jesus better, but you will be able to think of more. The better we know Jesus, the more we will experience him changing us and helping us to follow him, and we will be better equipped, too, to share the good news with our friends.

I pray that, as you let God use Mark's Gospel in your life, in your student group and in your church, you will re-discover Jesus.

Finally...

Being a Christian is about much more than just believing a message: it's about knowing Jesus, the Christ, the Son of God. I am convinced that this is one reason why Mark wrote his Gospel. He wants us to see Jesus more clearly.

And we can ask Jesus to open the eyes of our minds and hearts, as he opened the physical eyes of blind people in the Gospel (see 8:22-26; 10:46-52).

One day soon, all of us who know Jesus will see him in the glory which Peter, James and John saw at the transfiguration. And then we will be like him.

And with his help we can get to know this glorified Lord now.

Appendix 1:
How to organize and run The Mark Drama

The Mark Drama is a dramatic presentation of Mark's Gospel, in which every incident is included. There is more information about this on http://www.themarkexperiment.com. What follows here is simply designed to whet your appetite.

The Mark Drama is theatre-in-the-round and involves no costumes, props or microphones. There are two versions.

1. The Interactive Version

A group of between 40 and 120 Christians come together for a whole Saturday and divide into six groups. Each group is given one of the six sections of Mark. The group studies its section and decides how they will present it as drama to the whole group. They then practise their section (as theatre-in-the-round) until it runs smoothly.

The same evening all six groups come back together for **The Mark Drama**. After a short prayer asking the Lord for his help, the leader of the event narrates Mark's Introduction (1:1-8). Then, without any break, the first group presents Section One, then the second group presents Section Two, and so on. There is no break between the sections. At the end of Section Six the leader of the event narrates Mark's Conclusion (16:9-20). All this happens without the use of Bibles or notes. This is not difficult because each group knows its own section.

At the end of the Gospel there is a short time of worship and prayer.

For most people doing drama does not come naturally or easily, but the interactive version of **The Mark Drama** is a very powerful fellowship experience as everyone works together to achieve the aim of presenting the whole of Mark. I have found it best to make the performance an event only for those who are involved in the acting groups.

There is much more information about how to run the interactive version of **The Mark Drama** on the website.

2. The Team Version

This version of **The Mark Drama** involves a team of 15 people from a church or student group presenting the whole Gospel of Mark as theatre-in-the-round. This means that others are welcome to the performance: it is a fantastic opportunity to invite friends to experience the whole of the Jesus story. After the performance free copies of Mark are available to take away; perhaps people will be invited to Mark Discovery groups.

At least 2 months before the performance date there should be an information evening for all those who might consider joining the acting team and who want to know what commitment would be involved. If the necessary team comes together they have six weeks in which to learn the order of the events of the whole Gospel. This is not difficult if they use this book to help them.

There are only three rehearsals for **The Mark Drama**! The first is on Thursday evening, the second is on Friday evening and the third is on Saturday from 9am till 3.30pm. The performance takes place the same evening.

The team version of **The Mark Drama** is only possible with a director who has been trained and prepared. There are a number of such directors willing and able to lead information evenings and to direct the drama, and there are training days for people wanting to become directors themselves.

There is much more information about the team version of **The Mark Drama** on the website.

Appendix 2:
The Mark Experiment in a House-Group

The following series of studies lasts 13 weeks and is designed for group use. Many people find it easier to learn and use the Gospel if they are doing this with others.

Some hints for group leaders

1. The aim must be clear: we are doing the Mark experiment in order to get to know Jesus Christ better.

2. Try to create an atmosphere where people feel relaxed, so that they can enjoy learning by heart instead of being nervous about it.

3. It would be helpful to have a poster for each of the six sections, as well as for Mark's Introduction (1:1-8). The group can either copy down the section or everyone can have his or her own copy of *The Mark Experiment*.

4. The explanation of the structure of each section can be found in the book, under the heading "Enjoying the View".

5. It would be possible to make a break between Weeks 7 and 8, in order to review the first half of the Gospel.

6. Apart from prayer for personal needs and for the spread of the gospel in the world, the prayer-time can be used to pray through the section of Mark which the group have been studying.

7. It would be good to suggest a Mark Walk (see My Conclusion), either as a group or in twos or threes.

8. Pray for the group that doing the Mark experiment together will result in an encounter with Jesus.

Thirteen weeks in Mark's Gospel

Week One

Explanation of the experiment: present the structure of the Gospel using Section Two as an example (see My Introduction in *The Mark Experiment*).

Why learn the Gospel?

The aim of the experiment: to get to know Jesus better

Read Mark's Introduction (1:1-8).

Use the following questions to study the passage:

1. Why did Mark write his Gospel? What does he want to convince us of?

2. Why is John the Baptist so important in these verses?

3. What is most significant in the Malachi and Isaiah passages?

4. What is the most important thing about John's message?

5. The three main Old Testament passages in which God promises a new covenant are Jeremiah 31:31-34, Ezekiel 36:25-27 and Joel 2:28-32. Which of these passages do you think John the Baptist is thinking of here?

6. How does Mark want his readers to be feeling at the end of verse 8?

Learn Mark's Introduction in the group (i.e. the five headings).

Pray together.

Week Two

Who knows Mark's Introduction by heart?

Section One (1:9-3:12)

>   Explanation of the structure

>   Read the section together

>   Explanation of the structure again

Study the section, using the questions below:

Questions about Section One:

1. Why are people so enthusiastic about Jesus in this section?

2. What are the reasons for the Pharisees' decision in 3:6? (See 2:1-3:6)

3. How could we describe Jesus in this first section of the Gospel? What is his priority? What has that got to do with us?

4. The title of this section is The Message. How often does Jesus preach his message in the section? Why?

5. Why does Jesus perform miracles in this section?

6. In 1:16-20 Jesus calls his first four disciples. How do you think they felt at the end of the section, having seen and heard so much?

Learn the section together (beginning with Block B)

Encourage the group to use this in their own lives in the coming week

Pray together.

Week Three

Section One – getting to know it better

Who knows Section One by heart?

Are there questions about anything in the section?

Practise telling one another the stories

Study a few of the incidents more closely (if time)

Pray through the section, incident by incident

Week Four

Who still knows Mark's Introduction? Who knows Section One?

Section Two (3:13-6:6)

> Explanation of the structure
>
> Read the section together
>
> Explanation of the structure again

Study the section, using the questions below:

Questions about Section Two

1. Why did Jesus call the apostles?
2. Why might the disciples be feeling a bit insecure at the end of Chapter 3?
3. What encouragement for insecure disciples is there in the four parables?
4. The four miracles show that Jesus is Lord in four areas of life. In which? What can we learn from this?
5. How does Jesus react to opposition? Why?

Learn the section together (beginning with Block B)

Encourage the group to use this in their own lives in the coming week

Pray together

Week Five

Section Two – getting to know it better

Who knows Section Two by heart?

Are there questions about anything in the section?

Practise telling one another the stories

Study a few of the incidents more closely (if time)

Pray through the section, incident by incident

Week Six

Who knows Mark's Introduction? And Section One? And Section Two?

Section Three (6:7-8:30)

> Explanation of the structure
>
> Read the section together
>
> Explanation of the structure again

Study the section, using the questions below:

Questions about Section Three

1. The theme of Section Three is The Training. How often do we see Jesus training his disciples here?

2. Look at the sandwich in 6:7-33. What does the filling have to do with the bread?

3. The second sandwich in this section is in 8:14-30. What does the filling here have to do with the bread?

4. In 8:15 Jesus warns the disciples about the yeast of the Pharisees and of Herod. How does the section as a whole explain what Jesus means? And what can we do to take 8:15 seriously?

5. Does Jesus find it easy to train his disciples? How do you think he feels in 8:29?

Learn the section together (beginning with Block B)

Encourage the group to use this in their lives in the coming week

Pray together

Week Seven

Section Three – getting to know it better

Who knows Section Three by heart?

Are there questions about anything in the section?

Practise telling one another the stories

Study a few of the incidents more closely (if time)

Pray through the section, incident by incident

Week Eight

Who knows Mark's Introduction? And Section One?/Two?/Three?

Section Four (8:31-10:52)

> Explanation of the structure

Read the section together

Explanation of the structure again

Study the section, using the questions below:

Questions about Section Four

1. Why do you think the disciples don't understand what Jesus means when he predicts his suffering, death and resurrection?

2. Why are there only two miracles in this section? What do they have in common?

3. Look at the three mistakes of 9:33-50. Which of the three is the biggest danger for us today?

4. Why was the transfiguration a key event in the experience of Peter, James and John?

5. How do these three disciples behave in the rest of the section? How could we describe them?

Learn the section together (beginning with Block B)

Encourage the group to use this in their lives in the coming week

Pray together

Week Nine

Section Four – getting to know it better

Who knows Section Four by heart?

Are there questions about anything in the section?

Practise telling one another the stories

Study a few of the incidents more closely (if time)

Pray through the section, incident by incident

Week Ten

Who knows Mark's Introduction? And Section One?/Two?/Three?/Four?

Section Five (11:1-13:37)

Explanation of the structure

Read the section together

Explanation of the structure again

Study the section together, using the questions below:

Questions about Section Five

1. How could we describe the religious leaders in this section?

2. Who among the religious elite is the exception? What makes him different?

3. Try to imagine how Jesus feels in 12:6-8. And how do you think the religious leaders feel in verse 9?

4. Look at the sandwich in 11:12-25. What does the filling have to do with the bread? What was Jesus looking for in Israel? And what is he looking for in us?

5. Do you think hearing Jesus' words in Chapter 13 was a positive or a negative experience for Peter, James, John and Andrew?

Learn the section together (beginning with Block B)

Pray together

Week Eleven

Section Five – getting to know it better

Who knows Section Five by heart?

Are there questions about anything in the section?

Practise telling one another the stories

Study a few of the incidents more closely (if time)

Pray through the section, incident by incident

Week Twelve

Who knows Mark's Introduction? And Section One? / Two? / Three? / Four? / Five?

Section Six (14:1-16:8)

      Explanation of the structure

      Read the section together

      Explanation of the structure again

Study the section together, using the questions below:

Questions about Section Six

1. Which people in this section are loyal to Jesus? And which are not? Why?

2. Try to imagine Jesus' feelings during every incident in Section Six.

3. In what way does the Last Supper explain the meaning of the crucifixion?

4. Look at Jesus before the Jewish Council and then before Pilate. Which questions does he answer and which does he not answer? Why?

5. Why are the words "and Peter" in 16:7 important? What can we learn from this?

Learn the section together (beginning with Block B)

Pray together

Week Thirteen

Section Six – getting to know it better

Who knows Section Six by heart?

Read Mark's Conclusion together (16:9-20) and look at the three headings

Practise telling one another the stories

Study a few of the incidents more closely (if time)

Pray through the section, incident by incident

Appendix 3:
The Mirror Links in every Block B

Sometimes these links are more obvious, sometimes less so. Sometimes they point out similarities, and sometimes contrasts. You may not be convinced by all the links I suggest; I have simply collected the links here as far as I think I understand them. I am still learning!

Section One, Block B

a and a'	both happen on the Sabbath – with no opposition (a), and with opposition (a'). And in both incidents Jesus teaches with authority.
b and b'	the identity of Jesus (1:34 and 2:19).
c and c'	why Jesus has come – to preach (1:38) and to call sinners (2:17).
d and d'	both involve Jesus' relationship to official Judaism: submitting to it (d) and being attacked by it (d').

Section Two, Block B

a and a'	whenever the word of God is spoken, there are different responses (4:14-20 and 5:39-40).
b and b'	hidden things are uncovered (4:22 and 5:30-34).
c and c'	"Night and day" (4:27 and 5:5). The kingdom is constantly growing (c), but evil is constantly at work to destroy human beings (c').
d and d'	small beginnings lead to a great result one day. The small beginning in Incident d' may be the disciples' question (4:41), but some in the early church saw the boat as a picture of the church, which has seen amazing growth down the centuries.

Section Three, Block B

a and a'	the feeding of two huge crowds, one Jewish (a) and one Gentile (a').
b and b'	people are amazed at Jesus (6:51 and 7:37).
c and c'	Jesus can heal by personal contact (6:56) or at a distance (7:29-30).
d and d'	confrontation with the Jewish leaders

Section Four, Block B

a and a'   Jesus will die and rise again (9:31); disciples will suffer in this life but have eternal life in the next (10:30).

b and b'   status – important for the disciples (b) and for the rich young man (b'). Another link may be children (9:37 and 10:24).

c and c'   the disciples try to stop something happening, and Jesus tells them not to (9:39 and 10:14).

d and d'   the destructive power of sin (d), which can destroy marriages too (d').

Section Five, Block B

a and a'   the arrogance of the Jewish leaders (a) is contrasted with the humility of the widow (a'). All they have to offer is two questions designed to destroy Jesus; what she has to offer is two coins designed to glorify God.

b and b'   the severe punishment coming to the religious leaders (12:9 and 12:40).

c and c'   two unanswerable questions, one asked by the Jewish leaders (c) and one by Jesus (c'). (But Jesus manages to answer their question!)

d and d'   a dishonest question (d) is contrasted with an honest one (d'). The Sadducees do not know the Scriptures (12:24), while the teacher of the law does (12:32-34).

Section Six, Block B

a and a'   the last supper (a) explains the cross (a').

b and b'   the disloyalty of the disciples (b) is contrasted with the loyalty and steadfastness of Jesus (b').

c and c'   Jesus warns Peter of the dangers of prayerlessness (c); Peter demonstrates its results (c'). Jesus prays three times (c); Peter fails three times (c').

d and d'   the disloyalty of the disciples (d) is again contrasted with Jesus' steadfastness under pressure (d').

Appendix 4:
The Structure of Mark's Gospel

Mark's Introduction (1:1-8)

a   Mark's witness to Jesus (1)
b   The Old Testament prophets' witness to Jesus (2-3)
c   The baptism of John creates great interest (4-5)
b'   John is like an Old Testament prophet (6)
a'   John's witness to Jesus (7-8)

Section One: The Message (1:9-3:12)

Block A (1:9-20)
Baptism and temptation of Jesus (9-13)
Jesus proclaims the good news (14-15)
Jesus calls the first disciples (16-20)

Block B (1:21-2:28)

a	1:21-28	Jesus drives out an evil spirit
b	1:29-34	Jesus heals Peter's mother-in-law and others
c	1:35-39	Jesus says his priority is teaching
d	1:40-45	Jesus heals a leper
d'	2:1-12	Jesus heals a paralytic
c'	2:13-17	Jesus calls Levi and eats with sinners
b'	2:18-22	Jesus predicts a radical break with Judaism
a'	2:23-28	Jesus is Lord of the Sabbath

Block C (3:1-12)
Jesus provokes opposition by healing on the Sabbath (1-6)
Jesus' growing popularity (7-12)

Section Two: The Power (3:13-6:6)

Block A (3:13-35)
Appointing of the 12 Apostles (13-19)
Opposition from the family (20-21)
Opposition from the religious leaders (22-30)
Opposition from the family again (31-35)

Block B (4:1-5:43)

a	4:1-20	Parable: The sower
b	4:21-25	Parable: The lamp

c	4:26-29	Parable: The seed growing secretly
d	4:30-34	Parable: The mustard seed
d'	4:35-41	Miracle: Stilling of the storm
c'	5:1-20	Miracle: Driving out of Legion
b'	5:25-34	Miracle: Healing of a sick woman
a'	5:21-43	Miracle: Raising of Jairus' daughter

Block C (6:1-6)
Opposition from family and friends (1-6)

Section Three: The Training (6:7-8:30)

Block A (6:7-33)
Jesus sends out the Twelve (7-13)
The death of John the Baptist (14-29)
The Twelve return to Jesus (30-33)

Block B (6:34-8:10)

a	6:34-44	Feeding of the 5,000
b	6:45-52	Jesus walks on the water
c	6:53-56	Jesus heals in Gennesaret
d	7:1-13	God's word and human tradition
d'	7:14-23	What makes people unclean?
c'	7:24-30	Jesus and the Syro-Phoenician woman
b'	7:31-37	Jesus heals a deaf and dumb man
a'	8:1-10	Feeding of the 4,000

Block C (8:11-30)
The Pharisees demand a sign (11-13)
The confusion of the disciples (14-21)
The healing in two stages of a blind man (22-26)
Peter's confession of Jesus (27-30)

Section Four: The Cost (8:31-10:52)

Block A (8:31-9:29)
First prediction (8:31-33)
The call to discipleship (8:34-9:1)
The transfiguration (9:2-13)
Jesus drives out an evil spirit (9:14-29)

Block B (9:30-10:31)

a	9:30-32	Second prediction
b	9:33-37	"I am the greatest"
c	9:38-41	"We are the only ones"

d	9:42-50	"Sin doesn't matter"
d'	10:1-12	Attitude to marriage
c'	10:13-16	Attitude to children
b'	10:17-27	Attitude to possessions
a'	10:28-31	The rewards of discipleship

Block C (10:32-52)

Third prediction (32-34)

James and John's request (35-45)

The healing of blind Bartimaeus (46-52)

Section Five: The Judgment (11:1-13:37)

Block A (11:1-25)

Jesus enters Jerusalem (1-11)

Jesus curses the fig-tree (12-14)

Jesus clears the temple (15-19)

Jesus teaches lessons about prayer from the fig-tree (20-25)

Block B (11:27-12:44)

a	11:27-33	The authority of Jesus questioned
b	12:1-12	The parable of the tenants
c	12:13-17	Paying taxes to Caesar
d	12:18-27	Marriage at the resurrection
d'	12:28-34	The greatest commandment
c'	12:35-37	A question about the Messiah
b'	12:38-40	Warning about the teachers of the law
a'	12:41-44	The widow's offering

Block C (13:1-37)

The destruction of the temple and the end of the world (1-37)

Section Six: The Love (14:1-16:8)

Block A (14:1-11)

Plans against Jesus (1-2)

The anointing at Bethany (3-9)

Plans against Jesus (10-11)

Block B (14:12-15:39)

a	14:12-26	The last supper
b	14:27-31	Jesus predicts Peter's denial
c	14:32-42	Gethsemane
d	14:43-52	Jesus arrested
d'	14:53-65	Before the Jewish Council

c'	14:66-72	Peter denies Jesus
b'	15:1-15	Jesus before Pilate
a'	15:16-39	The crucifixion

Block C (15:40-16:8)
The women at the cross (15:40-41)
The burial of Jesus (15:42-47)
The resurrection (16:1-8)

Mark's Conclusion (16:9-20)

a	The appearances of the risen Lord (9-14)
b	The message of the sending Lord (15-18)
c	The disciples of the ascended Lord (19-20)

Motivating Generation X

THE POTENTIAL OF GENERATION X
AS A CHALLENGE FOR CHRISTIANS AND FOR MISSIONS

by

JÜRG PFISTER

"I am really praying that many people will read this futuristic, cutting-edge, strategic book. Let's make sure this book gets wide circulation."

George Verwer
Founder of Operation Mobilisation (OM)

"Hope and help: such can I best describe the book 'Motivating Generation X' by Jürg Pfister. I hope that 'Motivating Generation X' will be read by responsible members of congregations and missions boards, that it will be heard and that its corresponding initiatives will be implemented."

Thomas Bucher
President of the Evangelical Alliance of Switzerland

Once I had begun to read Jürg Pfister's book, I could not put it down.

Dr. Roland Werner, Germany

Paperback · 135 pp. · $12,99 / £10,95 / €12,80
ISBN 3-937965-06-8

VTR Publications
vtr@compuserve.com
http://www.vtr-online.de

Printed in the United Kingdom
by Lightning Source UK Ltd.
120464UK00001B/334-450